PREFACE

Professor Étienne Balazs had a strong claim to be the father of modern studies of China in Europe. Since the war he has exerted a very great influence on his younger colleagues, not only through his published writings, but perhaps even more by his concern—expressed in always trenchant and polemical terms—to focus their attention upon significant aspects of Chinese culture rather than upon subjects of marginal interest, and by his efforts to improve our methodology and to promote close scholarly contact between those engaged in Chinese studies in the various European centres. It is largely due to his personal influence that Chinese studies in Europe have begun to achieve some measure of integration into an academic field with a common sense of purpose and with ever-improving professional standards.

Those of us who began our professional careers in the fat post-war years would do well to reflect upon the circumstances under which Professor Balazs, like so many of his generation, produced his corpus of fundamental studies. Driven from country to country by the political upheavals and persecutions of pre-war Europe, he spent many years on the side-lines of sinology, and only late in life achieved a permanent academic appointment which could support him in reasonable comfort. A pioneer of modern historical studies of China, he was out-of-place in the pre-war world of sinology, for whose petty and parochial preoccupations and interests and for whose lack of any rigorous methodology he held a contempt which he never bothered to conceal.

His writings were concentrated on two main topics, the economic and institutional history of the period from the end of the Han dynasty until the end of the T'ang (roughly A.D. 200-900), and the history of Chinese political thought. It was perhaps in the former field that his achievement was the more substantial. His doctoral thesis for the University of Berlin, a brilliant analysis of the economic history of the T'ang period, was the first really professional study of

3

Chinese economic history in a Western language. Beside this and many later analytical studies, he leaves editions and translations of a number of basic texts on institutional history, some of them still unpublished, which demonstrate a rare mastery of documentary Chinese and medieval historiography.

In 1957, during his first visit to the Far East, he suffered a serious heart attack in Tokyo and for some years thereafter wrote very little. During these years he turned his attention more and more to the study of the recent centuries of Chinese history, and in particular to the study of the Chinese bureaucratic state. His interest in this subject was far from purely academic. He had a passionate and consuming personal involvement with political ideas, and these lectures in a sense crystallize his ambivalent attitude towards political theory and towards the impact upon the citizen of state power based upon such theory. He had a profoundly pessimistic vision of the vast gulf between political theory and the practice of government as he observed it in the present-day world, and for him the Chinese historical record confirmed his scepticism over the dichotomy between political ideal and social institution.

These three lectures were delivered in January 1963 at the invitation of the University of London. Professor Balazs died suddenly and unexpectedly of a second heart attack on 29 November, 1963, before he could finally edit them for publication. The versions printed here are substantially the lectures as he delivered them. Doubtless, had he lived, Professor Balazs would have developed these ideas further, but the lectures as they stand are of outstanding interest, and may perhaps stimulate some of his younger colleagues to continue his work on these fundamentally important historical themes.

The translation of the Ch'ing period manual on local administration, Hsüeh-chih i-shuo, upon which the last lecture is largely based, was left almost completed and it is hoped that it will be published in the near future.

D. C. TWITCHETT

CHINESE SEVENTEENTH-CENTURY
POLITICAL PHILOSOPHY

I

THE SEVENTEENTH CENTURY in Europe is crowded with meaningful names: from Cromwell to Colbert, from Galileo to Newton, from Descartes to Pascal and Leibniz, from Donne and Lope de Vega to Velasquez and Vermeer, there is a pleiad of giants who were instrumental in building Western civilization. But the seventeenth century in China is a blank, at least as far as the ordinary educated man in the West is concerned, and even the specialist is not aware of the tremendous consequences this age had for China and the whole of the Far East.

My thesis, then, is that the material and intellectual roots of modern China—or, if you prefer, of pre-modern China, in the sense of the pre-industrial China before the Western impact—are to be found in the seventeenth century, and that the trends which were to lead to that end-product of a very long evolution, the China of the Ch'ing dynasty, began to be operative during this century.

There are two main factors which went to the making of this pre-modern China. One is the infiltration of Western influences, which followed two lines of attack: (a) scientific thought (mathematics, astronomy, etc.) transmitted by the Jesuits; and (b) cannons, or in other words, power politics —the forceful opening of the huge country by war, occupation and colonization, as a result of the expansion of the European powers. The other moulding force is the autochthonous, self-bred movement of ideas, the main purpose, or at least the main outcome, of which was the freeing of Chinese thought from the shackles of scholastic philosophy and the fetters of the all-pervading *li-hsüeh*.[1] Now, while a certain amount is vaguely known about the first of these influences and some marginal studies of it have been made, the second has been entirely neglected in Europe, and even in China the study of it is far from satisfactory.

The indigenous liberation movement of Chinese thought

—let us state this in anticipation at the outset—went through four stages, each rising higher above the attainments of the foregoing. In the first stage, the holy scriptures —the venerated canonical writings of Confucianism—were taken seriously, Confucius was taken at his word, and a sincere attempt was made to realize all Utopian imperatives and return to antiquity. The inevitable disappointment of ingenuous faith led to a second, decisive stage: the critical dissection of the canonical texts. To question the scriptures and challenge their authority was a gigantic task. It demanded a combination of vast learning, patient, indefatigable, painstaking labours, and a bold, fearless revolutionary spirit. The achievement of a discipline of historical and *textual criticism* could not fail to lead to the rejection of a large part of the scriptures as being interpolated, altered, not genuine, or intentionally falsified. In turn, the effects of the purely textual criticism produced an attitude of distrust of all scriptural authority, an unconscious resistance and later a conscious rebellion against all antiquity, idealized or not, against the whole Confucian ethic, and finally against all tradition. This last stage was actually reached only at the end of the last and the beginning of this century.

We can distinguish several lines of force, or tracks along which the emancipation felt its way. The main road was certainly that of anti-traditionalism. It began with the rejection of Sung metaphysics and Ming philosophy, expanded into a rejection of the shallow erudition of these dynasties, and groped through Han learning back to the original sources of antiquity, the mainspring of knowledge. It is easy to see a parallel here with the return to the Greek classics in the European Renaissance. Another track is the anti-monarchist trend, others again, nationalism and democracy. These complex and contradictory cross-lines have a common denominator: anti-absolutism. They can only be disentangled if seen against the background of the end of a Chinese dynasty. And the end of this dynasty was of a peculiar nature, different from the normal death of Chinese dynasties. For the Ming dynasty, coming between the Mongols and the Manchus, was the last national dynasty, and the new barbarian Ch'ing dynasty that followed was to be not only the last of the barbarian dynasties, but the last of all dynasties. Of course, the actors of the age were not aware of this. Nevertheless, the seventeenth century, being the transition period between the Ming and the Ch'ing, allowed for a more rapid ripening of tendencies and tensions which would have been nipped in the bud in normal circumstances. It was easier to fight against absolutism and go nationalist under foreign occupation.

Finally there are two other trends, the most fertile of the whole movement. These were scientific research and historicism. The positive achievement of the seventeenth-century "School of Han learning" *(Han-hsüeh)*[e2] or "School of textual criticism" *(k'ao-cheng hsüeh)*[e3] was that it relied only on evidence that was subject to proof, that it rejected superstition, legendary tradition, and supra-rational revelations, that it considered every subject of learning to be not something immutable but something which underwent change as times changed, and that its members accepted without prejudice the results obtained by each and all of them in order to build up a solid body of knowledge.

The learned world of this time was also keenly interested in mathematics and natural science—it is significant that nearly all the great philosophers and historians were engaged in such studies. But it is only natural that the greatest achievements, which were truly scientific and of an astonishingly high quality even today, are to be found in those fields in which the scholars were primarily interested, namely, phonetics, etymology, and historical and textual criticism. It is often their unaffected artlessness, and the honest simplicity with which they groped in the dark, that give these men their charm and make us feel a warm affection for them.

But before presenting here three outstanding examples of the men of this fascinating age, let me say a word about the difficulties in studying it—which perhaps explain why there have been so few attempts to do so. First there is the difficulty presented by the amazing number of names. If the disparaging word *chinoiserie* may be permitted, this is certainly the right place to apply it. Every well-known man had, besides his family name, at least three other names: his *ming*, which was only used officially; his *tzu*, frequent in letters; and his *hao*, under which he wrote, and by which he was known among his disciples. In addition, most of them indulged in the habit of changing these three varieties of names several times, and it is not rare to find, particularly among artists and monks, up to a dozen or more names for one and the same person. Thus, in order to recognize references to say one hundred important persons of the period (and of course there were many more than a hundred), it is necessary to be familiar with about a thousand names.

Not only are their names numerous, but so are their works as well. The greatest difficulty, however, lies elsewhere. It lies in our ignorance of Ming history, a knowledge of which is required to provide the indispensable background to any problem raised; and—what is even worse—in our ignorance or false interpretation of the fundamental notions at stake in the philosophical and political fields. It is as if we were reading three-hundred-year-old leaders of the *Jen-min jih-pao* ("The People's Daily"), telling us that at present the real danger is not *dogmatism*—meaning Mao—but *revisionism*—meaning Khrushchev. If you are not accustomed to the secret language you are lost.

Let us now have a look at the environment of our philosophers. What may be regarded as the Chinese sixteenth century spanned the period from 1522 to 1620, and there was an accelerating development in every walk of life under the two unusually long reigns of Chia-ching (1522-66: Emperor Shih-tsung) and Wan-li (1572-1620: Emperor Shen-tsung). If we were to generalize, we could use three words to characterize the whole age: change, exchange, and differentiation.

First, economic change. The traditional self-sufficient natural economy became infested with the cancerous cells of a monetary economy. The slow spread of the "single whip system" (*i-t'iao pien-fa*)[a] became nation-wide (in 1581); that is to say, that instead of a cumbersome diversity of taxes in kind, everybody paid one single land-tax in money. Further, the long-drawn-out conversion of the salt tax into a money tax came to an end during the last years of Wan-li, and after 1617 salt was no longer stored in the State depots. Taxes being levied in money, everyone was obliged to go to market to sell and buy commodities and labour. Peasants poured into the cities to sell their products or to become traders and artisans, and there was a mushroom growth of new small market-towns (*shih-chen*).[05] Around 1565, an observer complains that during the last forty or fifty years everything has changed. Formerly one-tenth of the people were in the government offices and nine-tenths in the fields. But with ever-increasing taxes, everyone is leaving agriculture. There are now ten times as many servants as before, five times as many people supported by working in offices, three times as many merchants and artisans, and twice as many loafers. Even if we don't take this very Chinese way of handling figures at its face value, it no doubt reflects a very real and profound change. We have hundreds and hundreds of contemporary records which corroborate this. For example, Ku Yen-wu—one of the men who form the subject of these lectures—states (quoting a contemporary gazetteer of She-hsien, the famous town of the Hsi-an merchants in Anhwei) that wealth is for the most part being derived from the non-agricultural professions, and that there is a tendency towards polarization, the few rich becoming richer and the many poor poorer. Mammon prevails without any serious opposition, greediness and voracity go beyond all bounds, and even next of kin devour each other remorselessly.

It became necessary to exchange commodities in order to make money, and more and more people became involved in a market economy, from the independent artisan, who was gradually replacing the declining institution of State artisans, to the big landlord who rationalized his crops. To be sure, the greatest impetus came from the rising textile industry. Out of two million *mou* around Sung-chiang and Hu-chou, the biggest centres of the busy silk and cotton industries, half was planted with cotton. But the ever-growing demand required cotton from the north, where Honan became the centre where cotton was exchanged for manufactured goods from the south. There was an intensive traffic along the Grand Canal and the southeastern sea coast. In big cities like Peking, Nanking, and Hangchow, in the trading centres of Hopei and Shantung, and in the ports of Fukien and Kwangtung, the products of far-away provinces were exchanged: sugar, timber, and paper from Fukien, rice, pottery, and paper from Kiangsi (where 50,000 workers were concentrated in thirty paper plants at the end of the sixteenth century). Mining and smelting works also thrived. Sea trade, formerly hampered by Japanese pirates, grew brisk again. (Actually, Chinese merchants had never ceased to play quite an active part in trade throughout the long period when it was dominated by Japanese piracy.) From 1571 on, grain transport by sea was renewed, although already 12,000 ships were employed for grain transport along the Grand Canal. And of course there was also foreign trade. Chinese silk fetched five to six times the price in Japan, and Fuchow exported thousands and thousands of pieces of pottery to Nagasaki. Tea was transported to London by the Dutch, and Western watches, wool, wine, glass, and precious stones were imported into China. The State took an excise of twenty to thirty per cent from the sea trade, this tariff being levied in money from 1573 on; and according to Ku Yen-wu, this revenue covered half the total amount of government expenditure. Ports like Canton, Macao, and Ningpo depended entirely on foreign trade.

Stirring change and bustling exchange pervaded the whole empire, except for the north-western and southwestern provinces. But the movement was far from uniform. On the contrary, it created important regional differences. The *Wu-tsa-tsu*,[6] a famous description of China of about 1600, states that "the riches of the whole empire are assembled at the capital (Peking)", but it also immediately adds: "but half of them are produced in Chiang-nan"— i.e., in the provinces south of the Yangtse. Indeed, differentiation, which we chose as the third watchword of the age,

was at work everywhere. Compared to the booming indus-
trial area of southern Kiangsu and northern Chekiang,
other provinces, especially in the north-west and south-
west (Shensi, Kansu, Yünnan, Kwangsi), might be regarded
as underdeveloped. Again, the difference between the urban
and the rural population was becoming more marked.
Lastly, there was social differentiation between wage-earners
and employers, evident not only in the towns, but also in
the countryside.

This, then, is an outrageously simplified picture of what
might be called the golden century of early Chinese capitalism—for all the instances referred to of monetary, com-
mercial, and urban development compel us to speak of
capitalism (and even more certainly, of the appearance of a
bourgeoisie). I am aware of the present quarrels as to how to
christen this child, but I do not see what other name can be
given it if we take into account a quite coherent series of
events about which I should now like to make one or two
points.

First, there was a new cohesion among the townspeople
(*shih-min*).⁰⁷ The various urban social strata, composed of
merchants, tradesmen, artisans, shopkeepers, and labourers,
often made common cause with the urban gentry—the
patriciate (*shih-hao*),⁰⁸ in resistance against exactions, corruption, and arbitrary measures. Absolutism, through the
medium of its peculiarly docile and greedy instruments, the
plebeian eunuchs, soon had to wage war against the rebel-
lious cities. From 1596 on, there were two dozen major and
minor rebellions in the most important urban centres,
spread over a period of thirty years. Insubordination usually
started with a refusal to comply with the growing demand
for more taxes (the coffers of the State being empty, and
the eunuchs' greed insatiable), and soon degenerated into
an armed rising of the people, who frequently succeeded not
only in defying, but in expelling the hated officials. This
chapter of Ming history is known under the euphemism of
"the evil of the mining taxes" (*K'uang-shui chih pi* is the
title of Chapter 65 of the *Ming-shih chi-shih pen mo*),⁰⁹
because this was the pretext used by the eunuchs in their

tax-raising campaign. Let me illustrate the very complex relationship between the State, the eunuchs, and the merchants, by the following statement of the Minister for Public Works of about 1615 (taken from the second chapter of the *Kung-pu ch'ang-k'u hsü-chih*,[c10] a guide through the workshops and stores of this ministry):

> Formerly, there existed only regular payment of taxes, and apart from the fixed amount there were no bribes (*p'u-tien*,[c11] lit. bed-and-pillow money). . . . At present, expenses for bribes exceed regular tax payments, and the sufferings of merchants who are obliged to supply goods to the State are worse than being scalded. As soon as people know that they have been appointed (as suppliers), they are as frightened as a doe, shave their heads (to become monks) or jump into rivers, and find a thousand other tricks in order to escape. I have seen these things with my own eyes. Now, in the opinion of your Majesty's servants, *current requirements of goods for the State cannot be satisfied without merchants*, and if the shopkeepers undertake to supply the government with raw materials, they should only have to make regular deliveries. Besides, what is the origin of the bed-and-pillow money? Indeed, when the eunuchs of the Palace Directorate were supervising deliveries, they were indulgent only if bribes were paid, but if bribes were missing, they indulged in all sorts of blackmail and did not stop until they had sucked their victims dry.

The townsmen were probably far from being fully conscious that they had their own particular interests to defend. But they were almost certainly aware of a feeling of dumb resentment against the behaviour of their oppressors and against the ideas of the ruling class in general.

More emphatic still was their need for entertainment, for something more exciting than the tedious moralizing homilies of Confucian schoolmasters. They wanted to hear about their own problems, to see on the stage actors embodying their own roles in life. But they themselves lacked the necessary skill and education, and they had to rely on members of the educated class to be their spokesmen. These deserters from the enemy camp—I think the expression is not exaggerated—set about creating a new form of literature, and earned their living by writing, illustrating, and editing novels and short stories. The sudden birth and enormous output of this new genre precisely in the most developed urban area in and around Suchow cannot be an accident. And what makes it even more probable that the new form of literary expression was linked with the needs of the new social strata is the realistic, naturalistic, and erotic character of the literature and art of the late sixteenth and early seventeenth century. What is more, the best recension of the *Shui-hu-chuan*,[c12] the novel recounting the exploits of forest outlaws who played the role of knight-errants—today a classic, but at the time a risky venture—was written by the great heretical philosopher and freethinker, Li Cho-wu (Li Chih,[c13] 1527-1602), who was an acquaintance of Matteo Ricci, and who, tried for immorality and subversive ideas, committed suicide in prison. *Chin-p'ing-mei*,[c14] the famous erotic novel about the everyday life of a well-to-do business man bent on dissipation and sensual pleasures, is attributed to the great literary figure, Wang Shih-chen[c15] (1526-90), and was published in Suchow about 1609. The great story collections known as *San-yen* (by Feng Meng-lung,[c16] 1574-1646), *P'ai-an ching-ch'i* (by Ling Meng-ch'u,[c17] 1580-1644), and *Chin-ku ch'i-kuan*[c18] appeared respectively at the following dates: 1620-27, 1628 and 1633, and between 1633 and 1644. Li Li-weng (Li yü,[c19] 1611-1680?), dramatist, poet, and essayist, and one of the most engaging personalities of the seventeenth century, who travelled all over China with a troupe of singing girls, and who was entirely dependent on his pen, was the author of another erotic novel (*Jou-p'u-t'uan*,[c20] 1634), the German translation of which recently caused a scandal in Switzerland. Another highly interesting writer Chin Sheng-t'an (Chin Jen-jui,[c21] 1610?-1661)—and even more symptomatic, because he was the acme of heresy—was executed for high treason in 1661. A conscious rebel against conventional literature, he dared to place the novel *Shui-hu-chuan* and the play *Hsi-hsiang-chi*[c22] on a par with the works of Ch'ü Yüan, Chuang-tzu, Ssu-ma Ch'ien and Tu Fu as outstanding examples of the Chinese genius. And Chin Sheng-t'an was a native of Suchow. All this goes to prove the second point I wish to make—namely, that the origin of this form of literature, written mainly in colloquial language, and un-Confucian or anti-Confucian in outlook, was primarily bourgeois.

The third point concerns the effervescence of the political scene. The ceaseless activity of factions and clubs bears witness to the restlessness of the time. Young literati—impassioned, enthusiastic, daring, and eager for martyrdom—gathered under the glorious banner of the persecuted Tung-lin party, with all its numerous branches and substitutes, and fought a harassing guerilla against the authorities. If one of their clubs or academies (*shu-yüan*)[c23]—those educational institutes which were bulwarks of public morality and hotbeds of political opposition—was forbidden, they went underground and founded a new one. It is, however, extremely difficult to get a clear picture of the issues involved, because the real issues had to be expressed in veiled terms, and it is now only possible to glimpse them obliquely in the attitudes of the class of scholar-officials, who vaguely knew against whom they had to take sides, but who were rather lost when it came to the question of what action to take. Reduced to its simplest terms, their platform may be described as follows: the enemy is absolutism, that is to say, the badly-advised emperors surrounded by vile eunuchs, who are the arch-enemy; let us have good emperors who, in a purified atmosphere, under the guidance of morally irreproachable men—in other words, of the we-group of righteous scholar-officials—will lead the country to a glorious renewal. I think this idea of *renewal* or *renaissance* is a leading one, because one of the foremost clubs bore the name of *Fu-she*.[c24] This originally referred to the renewal of ancient learning, but it is fairly certain that the members of the *Fu-she*—and all three of the philosophers of whom I shall speak belonged to it in their youth—interpreted renewal in the sense of a general renaissance, implying the regeneration of society as a whole.

One last point. The age was characterized by a combination of sophistication, eccentricity, and a seeking after sensual pleasures, covering a wide range of sometimes contradictory feelings and ideas. It is possible to speak of a combination of these three tendencies because, for one thing, many individuals either passed through phases of one or other of them or even combined all three at the same time; and for another, because all three were manifestations of a basically *non-conformist* spirit. The iconoclasm of the *K'uang-ch'an*[c25] sect—the mad, unkempt Ch'an monks whose goal was sudden enlightenment—and that of the Southern School of landscape painting which sought self-expression unhampered by trifling details, were both represented in the circle of Tung Ch'i-ch'ang[c26] (1555-1636), the wealthy grand seigneur who had a genius for painting and art collecting. Both the sect and the school of painting were "the result of long periods of suffocating refinement" (of the leisured class), as Professor Nelson Wu remarks in his recent study on Tung Ch'i-ch'ang,[1] where he quotes the post-1644 confession of one of those "jouisseurs" whose lives were spent in the enjoyment of sensual pleasures, extravagance, and luxury. This man became a hermit in his latter days, and his repentance is all the more striking when we learn that "he earned early fame for his taste in exquisite houses, beautiful women, and art, as well as for being a connoisseur of spring water for tea". His confession runs as follows:

> Now I am a man without a country and without a family. I have no place to go but into the wilderness of the mountains with my hair unbraided, looking as terrible as a wild man. . . . Thinking in repentance of the luxurious days in my noble family, I am going to wear a bamboo helmet over my head and put bamboo buckets on my feet instead of hairpin and shoes. I shall do this in repentance of my past extravagance. There will be quilted cotton clothing instead of fur, and hemp instead of fine weave, wild vegetables instead of meat, coarse grain instead of the usual rice, to repay for the light and warm garments that I wore and the sweet delicacies that I have consumed. A straw mat will be

my bed, and a stone my pillow; I shall enjoy no warmth or softness. . . . When I travel, I shall go on foot and shoulder my own bags; there will be no more servants.[2]

The translator rightly stresses the point that such confessions "throw into high relief *the surprising lack of awareness* (italics added) among people of the late Ming period that the end was near for their weary and weakened government and society".

Let us glance now, not at the government, which was of no significance, but at the court of the last emperors—a true cross-section of the crumbling society. What a portrait gallery, worthy of the pen of a Saint-Simon! The despotic Wan-li emperor,[c27] Shen-tsung, amateur of art and collector of ceramics, was only interested in the luxuries of palace life and the supply of money required for it, and stubbornly refused to have any contact with his ministers and officials, who were anxious to secure his succession. His unloved eldest son, whom he finally named his heir apparent and who finally reigned for only one month, was the subject of three sensational political trials staged by the anti-eunuch party. These were the so-called "club case",[c28] in which a mysterious attempt on his life when he was crown prince was atoned for by the execution of two eunuchs; the "red pill" case,[c29] in which an attempt was made to find out who was responsible for the short illness and sudden death of the one-month emperor; and a third case,[c30] which to all appearances was a crushing defeat for the eunuchs and seemed to spell the end of palace intrigues. A fifteen-year-old grandson of Emperor Shen-tsung was triumphantly rescued from the guardianship of an imperial consort and put on the throne. But in the end it was the terrible Wei Chung-hsien,[c31] the eunuch who governed in his name, who triumphed. The young emperor had been brought up by his nurse and by a eunuch, and, being quite illiterate, spent his short life working enthusiastically at his carpenter's bench. The five children of the imperial carpenter had died in infancy, and another grandson of Shen-tsung succeeded him—a weak young man known to history under three different temple names. In spite of his good intentions, he was incapable of changing the destiny of his dynasty; and when the country had fallen into utter chaos due to the risings of peasant-bandits within and the assaults of the Manchu barbarians from without, the last Ming emperor in desperation staged a dramatic suicide in Peking, whereupon the city was occupied by Li Tzu-ch'eng^{c32} (1605-45), one of the peasant leaders.

For the next twenty years the hopes of the loyalists were continuously disappointed. The southern courts of five Ming claimants to the throne were moved time and again, from Nanking to Fuchow, from Kwangtung to Kwangsi and then to Yünnan and Burma, and from Chekiang to Fukien and Chusan and Chin-men. They, too, form a strange gallery, these princes, who had only this in common: their perpetual blindness to the facts of the situation, the perpetual petty intrigues in their entourages, and their perpetual peregrinations. One of them, the Prince of Kuei,^{c33} adopted the Christian faith during the course of his wanderings, as did his whole family. Surprisingly enough, it was a eunuch who had been instrumental in this conversion. Two other scions of the imperial house who belonged to the Ming loyalists are two of the greatest artists of the seventeenth century—those "mad-Ch'an" monks and extraordinarily gifted painters, Shih-t'ao and Pa-ta-shan-jen.^{c34}

This, then, was the atmosphere—of a world out of joint —in which the men who were to undertake the re-evaluation of their shattered universe grew up. The first of the three I have selected is Huang Tsung-hsi^{c35} (1610-95), better known under his *hao* as Huang Li-chou. After the long introduction I have given you, it will be easy to understand the brief outlines of his biography. He was born in Yü-yao, in eastern Chekiang. When he was fifteen years old (I am counting *à la chinoise*—that is to say, according to Western counting he was only fourteen), he used to listen to the secret discussions of the Tung-lin party at his father's house in Peking, where his father held a post as a censor. This was at the time when Wei Chung-hsien's clique had begun taking prompt action against their opponents, and the persecution was at its worst—a time of terror described by a friend of Tung Ch'i-ch'ang when he said: "We survived by pretending to be deaf and dumb." In 1625, the year in which Huang's father was dismissed, six "gentlemen" were beaten to death in prison, among them the man who had dared to make a public accusation against Wei Chung-hsien as having committed twenty-four crimes. The next year, the revengeful bill of indictment against those who had arranged the three anti-eunuch trials was published, and many people, including Huang's father, were arrested and executed, while others, such as the leader of the Tung-lin party, committed suicide. (Before his death, Huang's father had introduced him to a teacher, the renowned philosopher Liu Tsung-chou[c36] (1578-1645), of the school of Wang Yang-ming.) These events spurred Huang Li-chou to patriotic deeds. Bearing in mind the quotation from the *Tso-chuan*[c37] which his grandfather had written, as a permanent reminder of the duty of revenge, on the walls of the family residence,[3] he never forgot who had murdered his father, and played a frantic part in the turmoil of events. He tried to stab the man who had been the public prosecutor at his father's trial, and to take vengeance against another man. He published a list of the descendants of the persecuted martyrs; and in Nanking he joined the *Fu-she*, which, significantly enough, was also called the Little Tung-lin (*Hsiao Tung-lin*).[c38] This "Party of Renewal" organized big meetings in the lower Yangtze delta, and tried to influence the nomination and dismissal of officials and the civil service examinations. In 1629, when, after the suicide of Wei Chung-hsien, a black list of about 400 names was drawn up denouncing the creatures of the fallen eunuch, one of Wei's allies, the dramatist and bon-vivant Juan Ta-ch'eng,[c39] handed in his resignation and retired to Nanking, where he tried to win over the young men belonging to the newly founded literary clubs. In order to crush the corrupting activities of this man, Huang conceived and organized the publication of the so-called *Nanking Manifesto*,[c40] signed by 140 members of the Fu-she. Juan Ta-ch'eng, now once more a minister (this time at the court of the Prince of Fu,[c41] the first of the pretenders after the fall of Peking), thought the moment was propitious for the arrest of the 140 signatories. But Huang Li-chou was elsewhere, actively engaged in organizing anti-Manchu resistance and guerilla warfare. First he went, with his teacher, to Hangchow, and then organized volunteers in Shao-hsing, where he met the Prince of Lu,[42] another pretender. After the voluntary death of his teacher (Liu Tsung-chou was one of the many people who, in 1645, despaired of seeing the Ming restored, and refused food and drink until they died), we find Huang building barricades in Chekiang, and later on in Chusan, where he joined the Prince of Lu.

And here, in the year 1649, Huang's political activities ended. He resigned, and retired into private life, subsequently refusing all offers of employment made by the Manchu régime. I should like to lay stress on this point, because we find the same feature in the biographies of other contemporaries. They are divided into two: the first part filled with feverish political activities, and the second part— longer, more important, but uneventful, and silent about public affairs—being the period of creative work. You can't understand the one without the other.

If we wish to avoid a tedious enumeration of Huang Li-chou's works (64 titles in 1,322 chapters (*chüan*), many of which remain unpublished), three sentences will serve to describe the second, creative period of his life. He entertained friendly relations with a few of his colleagues and paid visits to them. In 1662, the year which can be regarded as marking the beginning of the stabilization of the Ch'ing dynasty (the K'ang-hsi era lasted from 1662 to 1721), he wrote the *Ming-i tai-fang lu*,[43] his political testament. In 1676 he finished his magnum opus, the *Ming-ju hsüeh-an*[44] (62 chapters), the *acta eruditorum* of the Ming dynasty and actually the first history of Chinese philosophy—a work which excited nation-wide interest and which can be considered as the foundation-stone of the Chekiang school of historians (*Che-tung hsüeh-p'ai*),[45] that group of brilliant scholars, the most famous of whom was Chang Hsüeh-ch'eng[46] (1738-1801).

The work we are concerned with here is the *Ming-i tai-fang lu*, a political treatise. The title, which contains an allusion to the thirty-sixth hexagram of the "Book of Changes" (*I-ching*), means: waiting in the "brightness obscured" for the visit of an enlightened prince seeking for advice, and can perhaps best be rendered by "Propositions for a more propitious age". It is a systematic survey and critique of imperial institutions as they appeared in late Ming times, and deals with every important aspect of the Chinese State: administration and law, education, civil service (2), land system, military organization, taxation, and currency (three articles each), clerks and eunuchs (two paragraphs).

The first essay, "On the origin of princes" (*Yüan-chün*),[c47] which is full of Taoist terms, contains a frontal attack on despotism:

> In the beginning of human life each man lived for himself (*tzu-ssu*)[c48] and sought to benefit himself (*tzu-li*).[c49] There was such a thing as the common benefit, yet apparently no one promoted it; and there was common loss, yet apparently no one eliminated it. Then a man appeared who did not think of benefit in terms of his own personal gain, but sought to benefit all under Heaven; and who did not think of loss in terms of his own personal disadvantage, but sought to spare all under Heaven of loss. Thus his labors were thousands of times greater than the labors of ordinary men, ... (so) in those early times some men ... refused to become princes ... others undertook it, and then quit —Yao and Shun, for instance. Still others, like Yü, became princes against their own will.... However with those who later became princes it was different. They believed that since they held the power over benefit and loss, there was nothing wrong at all in taking for themselves all the benefits and leaving to others all the loss. They made it so that no man dared to live for himself or seek to benefit himself. Thus the prince made his own private interests the common end of all.... He looked upon the world as an enormous

estate to be handed on down to his descendants, for their perpetual pleasure and well-being. . . . In ancient times *the people were considered hosts (chu:* master, lord) *and the prince was the guest (k'o:* servant, tenant).*[c50] All of his life the prince spent working for the sake of the people. *Now the prince is host and the people are guests.* Because of the prince people can find peace and happiness nowhere. In order to achieve his ends, people must be harmed and killed and their families broken up—all for the aggrandizement of one man's fortune. Without feeling the least pity for mankind, the prince says: "I want only to establish this estate for the sake of my descendants." Yet when he has established it, the prince still wrings every drop of blood and marrow from the people and takes away their sons and daughters to serve his excessive pleasures. . . . Thus *the greatest enemy of mankind is the prince and nothing but the prince. If there had been no rulers, each man would have lived for himself and secured what was to his own benefit.* . . . Now men hate their prince and think of him as *a mortal foe . . .* and this is certainly what he deserves.[4] (Italics added.)

All this rings more radical than it really is, or rather, is more radical than the conclusions drawn by the author. The problem as to how far-reaching was the radicalism or the democracy or the land-reform or indeed every other issue raised by Huang Li-chou—and this is a question which crops up all the time, and to which his naïve admirers and mean detractors provide contradictory answers—can only be objectively and adequately solved if we bear in mind the following points. First, the limitations imposed on Huang's thought by his Confucian outlook, his social environment, and the society and age he lived in, should not be allowed to lessen his stature and reduce his merits. Indeed, it would be childish and absurd to expect to find a Western system of Parliamentary constitutional government, with checks and balances and so on, advocated by a Chinese thinker of the seventeenth century. Secondly, Huang had to be extremely careful about his use of language if he wanted his ideas to be diffused. This is especially true of all passages susceptible of being interpreted as anti-Manchu. Thirdly, Huang was certainly less radical, less extremist, than many of his contemporaries who either would not or could not express their ideas. Last but not least, Huang, far from being consistent and single-minded, is full of contradictions, inconsistencies, and emotionally Utopian wishful thinking. Who is not? And this last point is amply confirmed if we compare the Confucian, hopelessly "old stuff" title of his book with the pugnacious republicanism of the first chapter, and that again with the gentle tone, the prudent and sometimes timid reformism of other chapters. Judgments may, of course, vary according to the way in which various passages are interpreted. For instance, the first sentence asserting the right to individual happiness for everyone seems to me to be perhaps more remarkable than the famous tirade on the meanness of princes.

The ideas set forth in the second and third paragraph of "On the origin of ministers" (*Yüan-ch'en*)[51] and in the essay "On the origin of law" (*Yüan-fa*)[52] are in disagreement with the traditional Confucian conceptions. In the first, he writes:

> ... the world (*t'ien-hsia*) is too big for one man to govern and it is necessary to share the work with others. ... The governing of the world is like the hauling of great logs. The men in front call out "Heave!" and those behind "Ho!" The prince and his ministers are log-haulers working together. If some of them, instead of holding tight to the ropes with feet firmly set on the ground, amuse themselves by cavorting around in front, the others behind will think it the thing to do, and the business of hauling logs will be neglected. Alas, the insolent princes of later times indulge themselves [in the same way],* and do not attend to the business of the world and its people. From among the men of the country they seek out only such as will be servile errand-boys. And if from the country only those

---

* Square brackets are interpolations of the authors quoted, round brackets are Professor Balazs' own.

respond who are of the servile errand-boy type, then when they are protected from cold and hunger for a while, they feel eternally grateful for his majesty's kindness. Such men will not care whether they are treated with due respect, and will think it no more than proper to be relegated to a servant's status . . . princes and ministers differ in name only, and are in fact the same. . . . The terms "prince" and "minister" derive their significance from their service to mankind. If I have no sense of duty to mankind then I am an alien to the prince. If I come to serve him without any consideration for the welfare of mankind, then I am merely the prince's *menial servant*. If, on the other hand, I have the people's interest at heart, then I am the prince's *mentor and colleague*. Only then may I really be called a minister.[5] (Italics added.)

The real meaning of this claim that power should be shared as between partners can only be understood in the light of the last chapters on eunuchs, where Huang explains their disastrous influence in the Ming state as being due to their slave status. As docile and absolutely dependent instruments they complied with every whim of their imperial masters, and were encouraged to do so by the unworthy behaviour of civil officials, servility being contagious. I may add that the only solution offered by Huang was a drastic cut in the number of eunuchs—a very poor remedy.

The chapter on law, on the other hand, seems to me quite outstanding, not so much because he attached more importance to institutions than to the men administering them —others did this before him—as because of his illuminating analysis of law in Chinese society. I should like to quote this passage. After speaking about the ideal institutions of antiquity, he goes on:

The looser the law was, the fewer the disturbances which arose. It was what we might call "law without laws" (*wu-fa chih fa*).[53] The laws of later times safeguard the world as if it were something in the [prince's] treasure chest. It is not desired that anything beneficial should be left to the lowly, but rather that all blessings be reserved for the one on high. If the prince employs a man, he is immediately afraid that the man will act in his own interest, and so another man is employed *to keep a check on the first one. If one measure is adopted, there are immediate fears of its being abused or evaded, and so another measure must be adopted to guard against abuses or evasions.* All men know where the treasure chest lies, and the prince is constantly fretting and fidgeting out of anxiety for the security of his treasures. Consequently, the laws have to be made more comprehensive and detailed, and as they become more detailed, they become the very source of disorder. These are what might be called "unlawful laws" (*fei-fa chih fa*).[54] ... If it should be said that there are only men who govern well, not laws which govern well, my reply is that only if there are laws which govern well, will there later be men who govern well.[6] (Italics added.)

For those interested in the periodization of Chinese history, I should point out that in this essay and in several other places in the *Ming-i tai-fang lu*, Huang speaks of two great turning points in Chinese history: Ch'in Shih-huang, and the Mongol Yüan dynasty, the first marking the abolition of feudal antiquity, and the second the suppression of Chinese national institutions.

Huang's views on land reform are a strange mixture of Utopian beliefs and up-to-date factual information and statistical evidence. He believed in the feasibility of adopting the ancient *ching-t'ien*[55] or well-field system. Now we must be clear as to what advocating the *ching-t'ien* system really meant in imperial China: it simply meant advocating land reform. Everyone took it for granted that the system really had existed in ancient times, and there were three possible attitudes that could be adopted towards it. The overwhelming majority of Confucian scholar-officials, themselves landlords, admired the venerable institution, but held that what was possible or good for the times of Confucius was no longer feasible. The second attitude, which was the one adopted by Huang and a few other liberal-minded men, was to regard the redistribution of land as something that was both necessary and possible to carry out. The third attitude consisted of breaking free from Utopias and ancient precedents and demanding social action for the redistribution of the big estates. But only illiterate peasants, unaffected by tradition, thought in this way. This question, however, does not concern us here. In short, Huang took the military agricultural colonies as evidence of the feasibility of putting the *ching-t'ien* system into operation, and showed neatly, using the available official figures provided by the *Ming Hui-tien*[56] of 1578, that the 700 million *mou* under cultivation when divided among the nearly 11 million households of the empire, would provide fifty *mou* each (corresponding exactly to the ritual 100 *mou* of antiquity), and there would still be more than 170 million *mou* left over. What, then, should happen to this remainder? Let me quote again, this point being of great importance:

> If the rich were allowed to occupy the remainder, no one need feel that he did not have enough. So why must there be any fuss over property limitations and equalization of land, or this needless to-do about causing the rich to suffer?[7]

You see, Huang is a very "reasonable", moderate land reformer, on his guard against the obvious accusation of being a leveller, which he certainly was not.

Nor did he see the real implication of the silver tax. He recommended the adoption of a mixed system of paper money and copper cash, and the abolition of silver as currency. On the other hand, in his essays on land and finances, he is extremely clearsighted about the evils of the exploitation of the peasantry through constant accumulation of taxes and constant commutation of taxes from kind to money and from money to kind, according to the interests of the Imperial Treasury. There is no time to go into details.

Unquestionably, Huang Li-chou's most original contribution are his proposals concerning schools and education. He wished to create a universal public school system with a purpose going far beyond the training of officials. Indeed,

the ideal school should be the centre and the most important organ of the community, providing an education for
everybody and acting as an organ for the free expression of
public opinion—a kind of popular parliament. This
original conception had a twofold aim: that of inculcating
the desired political opinions in the State schools, while
removing the subversive political trends of the *shu-yüan*.
This conception can only be understood against the background of late Ming times, when the State schools no
longer fulfilled their function of training scholars for office,
but had more and more become a lifeless machine of
conformism which every year turned out a fixed quota of
third-rate people who could say yes and could write "eight-
legged" essays which nobody could read and even examiners
did not care for. At the same time, the private institutes of
learning, the *shu-yüan* (usually called academies), where
the sons of scholar-officials flocked in large numbers, had also
lost their educational function and had more and more
become centres of political opposition, in open conflict
with the State, which tried to silence and suppress these
dens of dissent, heterodoxy, heresy, and insubordination.
Let us hear the relevant passage from the essay on schools
(*hsüeh-hsiao*)[57]:

> What the Son of Heaven approves is not necessarily
> right and what he disapproves is not always wrong. [In
> ancient times] the emperor did not dare to determine
> right and wrong for himself, and left to the schools
> the public determination of right and wrong. There-
> fore, education of the literati is one of the tasks of
> schools, but schools are not only established for the
> education of literati. After the Three Dynasties, right
> and wrong in the whole empire have been determined
> entirely by the court. If the Son of Heaven favoured
> such and such, everyone hastened to proclaim it right;
> if he frowned upon such and such, everyone con-
> demned it as wrong. The keeping of public records
> and making of annual reports, state finances, military
> and judicial affairs—all were left to petty civil em-
> ployees. There were, indeed, a few who escaped the

evil tendencies of the times, but they were apt to think the schools of no consequence in meeting the needs of the day. In their view the so-called schools merely joined in the mad scramble for office through the examination system and allowed themselves to become infatuated with ideas of wealth and noble rank. Finally, because of the seductive influence of the court, there was a complete change in the qualifications of school-men. Those scholars who had real ability and learning came more and more from the countryside, having nothing to do with the schools from start to finish. So, in the end, the schools failed even in the one function of training scholars. Thereupon the schools were replaced by private institutes of learning. If these institutes were wrong, you can be sure the government approved and honoured them; if they were good, the government condemned and disgraced them without fail. The interdiction of heretical doctrines and the destruction of private institutes of learning finally led to the determination to challenge the authority of the State.[8]

Now what were Huang's practical propositions? First, a thorough reform of the curriculum, introducing, in addition to the classics, non-Confucian philosophy (including Lao-tzu and Chuang-tzu), the dynastic histories and the *Ming-shih-lu*, and contemporary problems, as topics for the examinations. Second, candidates should offer their own interpretation of a question, taking into account all commentaries of the classics. Third, students of astronomy and medicine must go through a severe training before being employed. Doctors should be rated according to the number of births and deaths occurring in the cases under their care and the number of cures they can be shown to have effected. The lower class must be dismissed, the middle class can continue to practise, and the upper class can enter the Medical College. Fourth, in addition to examinations, other methods of selection based on administrative capacity should be adopted. Fifth, Buddhist and Taoist monasteries should be transformed into *shu-yüan* and the monks and nuns secularized, although they can study if they wish, and the income from the expropriated church lands should be used for the support of poor students. And here are the most important measures concerning the public schools generally, aptly summarized by Professor de Bary:

> There are to be schools from the capital down through every city and town to even the smallest hamlets, but on each level supervision is to be independent of control from above. The principal units of administration, the prefectures and districts, will be presided over by superintendents of education chosen locally, not appointed by the court. These men need never have served as officials before or qualified for civil service. Not only should they have complete freedom in ordinary educational matters, including the right to override the provincial commissioner of education in the appointment of licentiates [those who have achieved the first degree in the prefectural examinations], but their pronouncements on any matter affecting the community should be listened to respectfully by the local magistrates. Similarly, at the capital the libationer [or chancellor] of the Imperial Academy should lecture each month on important questions, with the emperor and his ministers attending in the role of students. In addition, the local superintendent is to have wide authority over other aspects of community life—public ceremonies, family ritual observances, censorship over publications, and public entertainment.[9]

There are many other remarkable details in this essay on schools, which is the boldest essay in the whole work. Two of the points made seem to me to deserve special emphasis. The first is that students should have the right to go on strike and refuse to study under any superintendent of education who had committed the slightest offence against moral standards of probity, and that if a local magistrate should treat old schoolmasters in an overbearing or contemptuous manner, the men of letters of the district should raise an uproar and get rid of him. The second point I would emphasize is the proposal to burn the printing blocks of that jumble of metaphysical conversations known as the *Yü-lu*,[c58] and of various ponderous and useless collections of memorials to the throne and examination essays. But it should be noted that, in addition to these, Huang Li-chou also recommended the destruction of novels, short stories, and plays. I lay stress on these two points because they show that, while Huang's hostility to fiction clearly marks him as being out-of-date nowadays, his claim for the right of students to strike was something that was likely to endear him to the younger generation of later times, especially if it is also remembered that the same essay contains a lengthy vindication of the political fight of patriotic students under the Sung dynasty. And, indeed, Hu Shih cleverly appointed Huang Li-chou as the patron saint of the May the Fourth Movement of 1919. One final point—and this brings us to the end, today. These interconnections over the centuries have a wider aspect. Students have always appeared as active political leaders in times when a young and powerless bourgeoisie is claiming its rights. *Mutatis mutandis* we find the same forces at work whether it be in China at the end of Northern Sung or the beginning of the seventeenth century or the dawn of the twentieth, or in Europe in 1848. This explains why Liang Ch'i-ch'ao exhumed the *Ming-i ti-fang lu* towards the end of the Ch'ing dynasty and had several tens of thousands of copies printed, which circulated clandestinely as a most powerful and influential political tract for spreading democratic and republican ideas. This late adoption of Huang's ideas shows the backwardness of later reformers compared with the vigour and courage of the pioneers.

II

T HE BEST WAY to introduce Ku Yen-wu[c1] (1613-82), better known under his *hao* as Ku T'ing-lin (he, too, changed his name twice after 1644), is to quote from his famous letter to a friend about learning:

> It is a matter of great regret to me that for the past hun-
> dred odd years, scholars have devoted so much dis-
> cussion to the mind and human nature (*hsin* and

hsing,[c2] the main categories of the subjective intuition-ism of the Wang Yang-ming school of Neo-Con-fucianism), all of it vague and quite incomprehensible. ... Gentlemen of today gather a hundred or so followers and disciples about them in their studies, and though as individuals they may be as different as grass and trees, they discourse with all of them on mind and nature. They set aside broad knowledge and concentrate upon the search for a single, all-inclusive method; they say not a word about the distress and poverty of the world within the four seas, but spend all their days lecturing on theories of the "weak and subtle", the "refined and undivided" (*wei-wei ching-i chih shuo*).[c3] ... What then do I consider to be the way of the sage? I would say "extensively studying all learning"[1] (*po-hsüeh yü wen*),[c4] and "in your conduct having a sense of shame"[2] (*hsing-chi yu ch'ih*).[c5] Every thing from your own body up to the whole nation should be a matter of study. In everything from your personal position ... to all your comings and goings, ... you should have things of which you would be ashamed. This sense of shame before others is a vital matter. It does not mean being ashamed of your clothing or of the food you eat, but ashamed that there should be a single humble man or woman who does not enjoy the blessings that are his due. ... Alas, if a scholar does not first define this sense of shame, he will have no basis as a person, and if he does not love antiquity and acquire broad knowledge, his learning will be vain and hollow. These baseless men with their hollow learning day after day pursue the affairs of the sage, and yet I perceive that with each day they only depart further from them.[3]

Correct though this translation may be (it is not mine but Professor de Bary's), it perhaps does not entirely convey the nobility of tone and the sharpness of attack of the original. But it does give us the maxim adopted by Ku as a rule of conduct which he lived up to throughout his whole life.

He was born in K'un-shan, near Suchow. At the age of two he lost the use of one eye through smallpox. His father, who had failed several times in the provincial examinations, died when Ku was in his fourteenth year, and Ku was brought up by his foster grandfather, who taught him the first elements of history, and by his austere foster mother, who, after the fall of K'un-shan in the summer of 1645, starved herself to death rather than live under alien rule, expressing on her deathbed the wish that her adopted son would never serve the Manchus. Already three years before, at the age of thirty, Ku had joined the Renewal Society (*Fu-she*), and he later accepted an appointment at the Fukien court of the pretender Prince of T'ang. But very soon a family incident changed the whole course of his life. The Ku family, an old family of scholars and officials, possessed an estate of 800 *mou*, which was rented to a neighbour, who wanted to get possession of it. With the help of a slave of Ku's, this man accused Ku T'ing-lin of sedition. Five years later Ku had the slave drowned, for which crime he was imprisoned and flogged. After regaining his freedom, he was attacked by an assassin hired by the good neighbour. But the assassin failed to complete his job, and Ku escaped with being wounded. This private persecution, which happened to take place during that chaotic mid-century period when the patriots had begun to give up the hopeless cause of restoration, drove Ku from home. He went to the north and undertook restless wanderings through all the provinces. To escape from private persecution and find a livelihood was only a pretext. The real reason for his endless journeyings was quite different. Already before the fall of the dynasty he had begun, out of antiquarian interest, as historian and geographer, to collect data which he used in his later works. But *now*, after the barbarian invasion and the peasant uprisings, the pursuit of his interests had acquired a new and very much wider dimension. Indeed, Ku had two objects in view: to inspect personally the regions of peasant guerilla warfare, and to assess the strategic possibilities of the terrain for subsequent resistance. In 1662, the year in which Huang Li-chou composed his political treatise, Ku wrote the preface to his huge economic and strategic geography of China, the deservedly famous *T'ien-hsia chün-kuo li-ping shu*,[06] today a storehouse of information about late-Ming China, but which, despite two useful editions, cannot really be fully utilized so long as there is no index to its 120 chapters.

Several times between his journeys he made attempts to settle permanently. First in Shantung, then as an agricultural colonist with borrowed money in the far north, and finally at the age of sixty-five on a plot of 50 mou in northwest Shensi. In this year, 1677, he also paid his sixth and last visit to the tombs of the Ming emperors. Needless to say, these ritual visits to the imperial remains on the part of someone who never tired of attacking the spirit of Ming philosophy and institutions were not so much an obeisance to the defunct dynasty as a homage rendered to China's grandeur, a demonstration of patriotic loyalty to the home country. In a letter of about the same period he wrote:

> All those who pursue studies today are seeking only their own benefit, trying to succeed in the examinations. Those who go further and compose literary texts and write books, hoping to create something worthwhile that will survive, do it only for fame and nothing else, just like the men of letters during the three hundred years of the Ming.[4 and 67]

He refused, of course, as did Huang Li-chou and other patriots, to participate in the booby-trap examinations for literati advertised with much ado by the new dynasty, although the name chosen for these examinations (*po-hsüeh hung-tz'u*) contained his beloved motto of "Broad Learning" (*po-hsüeh*), and he rejected the request to join the learned commission in charge of writing the "Draft History of the Ming Dynasty" (*Ming-shih kao*).[08] He certainly was not likely to forget that twenty years earlier (1660) he had only narrowly escaped the fate of several hundred people who were put to death for having published, printed, or bought a privately written Ming History (the *Ming-shih chi-lüeh*),[09] and ten years later he was in prison for more than six months indicted with the authorship of an anti-Manchu tract.

Ku had more useful and far more serious things to do, in the fields of archaeology, epigraphy, geography, and history. On his last visit to his home province, he published (1667) the "Five Books on Phonetics" (*Yin-hsüeh wu-shu*),[c10] the foundation-stone of all phonetic, etymological, and philological researches to come, a masterly demonstration of the new scientific method based on evidence, and a model for the whole generation of Ch'ing scholars for whom historical phonetics was not an idle sport, a diverting pastime, but a useful tool, a sharp weapon in the long war waged to demolish the Canonical Scriptures. He had to finish a compendium of historical geography compiled from over a thousand sources (the *Chao-yü chih*,[c11] which was never printed, but of which two incomplete manuscripts are preserved). He had to complete his "Record of Daily Knowledge" (*Jih-chih lu*),[c12] a first short version of which he sent for criticism to Huang Li-chou, with whose political ideas he declared himself to be sixty to seventy per cent in agreement. The *Jih-chih lu*, his imperishable title to fame, a work widely read even today, is the ripe harvest of life-long study, research, and reflection on all problems concerning the China of the seventeeth century. It consists of carefully composed and painstakingly revised jottings and short essays on the Classics, on economics, government, and moral, religious, and social questions, on the examinations system, and on historical, philological, and literary problems. In its final form of 32 chapters, it was published (1695) in Fukien, after his death, which overtook the great traveller during one of his rovings through southern Shansi.

Now, after what I have just said about the man of "broad knowledge" and "a sense of shame", what is the claim of Ku T'ing-lin to be reckoned among political thinkers? To be sure, his outstanding achievement is not in this field. Nevertheless, I believe we should range him alongside Huang Li-chou and Wang Ch'uan-shan as being the most influential exponent, not only of modern, scientific scholarship, but also of new ways of political thinking. Ku's main idea was to regard local autonomy as a remedy for all the

evils stemming from overconcentration of power in absolutism. He considered one of the worst evils to be the
estrangement of the court and of the regular civil officials
from the people, whose affairs were handled by the un-
scrupulous petty bureaucracy of clerks who were familiar
with local conditions. The same complaint, couched in
different terms, was to be raised up until the end of the
nineteenth century. In the *Jih-chih lu* he writes, in a note
about prefectural administration:

> In later ages there appeared inept rulers who gathered all
> authority into their own hands. But the countless
> exigencies of government are so broad that it is quite
> impossible for one man to handle them all, so that
> authority then shifted to the laws. With this a great
> many laws were promulgated to prevent crimes and
> violation, so that even the greatest criminals could
> not get around them, nor the cleverest officials accom-
> plish anything by evading them. People thereupon
> expended all their efforts in *merely following the laws
> and trying to stay out of difficulty.* Thus the authority
> of the Son of Heaven came to reside *not in the officials
> appointed by the government but in their clerks and
> assistants.* Now what the world needs most urgently
> are local officials who will personally look after the
> people, and yet today the men who possess least
> authority are precisely these local officials. If local
> officials possess no authority and the grievances of the
> people are not made known to the higher authorities,
> how can we hope to achieve peace and prosperity and
> prolong the life of the nation?[5] (Italics added.)

He expounded his views in nine short essays entitled
Chün-hsien lun ("On the prefectural system"),[6] from which
I would like to quote the beginning, because there, as with
Huang Li-chou, we can see at once the shortcomings and
the strengths of seventeenth-century political conceptions:
pungency of diagnosis, weakness of therapeutics:

> If we understand why the feudal system (*feng-chien*)[c13]
> changed into the prefectural system (*chün-hsien*),[c14]
> we will understand also that as the prefectural system

in turn falls into decay it too must change. Does this mean that there will be a *return to feudalism*? No, *this is impossible*. But if some sage were to appear who could invest the prefectural system with the essential meaning of feudalism, then the world would attain order. ... Today the prefectural system has reached a point of extreme decay, but no such sage appears and people go on doing everything in the old way. Therefore with each day the people become poorer, China grows weaker, and we hasten down the road to ruin. Why is this? The fault of feudalism was its concentration of power on the local level, while the fault of the prefectural system is its concentration of power at the top. The sage-rulers of antiquity were impartial and public-minded in their treatment of all men, parcelling out land to them and dividing up their domains. But now the ruler considers all the territory within the four seas to be his own prefecture, and is still unsatisfied. He suspects every person, he handles every affair that comes up, so that each day detailed prescriptions, directives and written documents pile higher than the day before. On top of this he sets up supervisors, provincial governors and governors-general, supposing that in this way he can keep the local officials from tyrannizing over and harming the people. He is unaware that these officials in charge are concerned only in moving with *utmost caution so as to stay out of trouble* until they have the good fortune to be relieved of their posts, and are quite unwilling to undertake anything beneficial to the people. Under such circumstances how can the people avoid poverty and the nation escape weakness? If this situation is allowed to continue unchanged, I am positive that it will lead only to chaos with trouble increasing day by day. If, however, the position of local officials is accorded its proper dignity, and such officials are granted fiscal and administrative authority, if the post of supervisor is discontinued, the enticement of hereditary office held out to officials, and a method whereby they may select their own subordinates put into effect, this will achieve the goal of imbuing the prefectural system with the essential meaning of feudalism, and the decay that has come about in the last two thousand years can be remedied. Rulers hereafter will find that if they hope to improve the livelihood of the people and strengthen the power of the nation (*hou min-sheng, ch'iang kuo-shih = fu-min ch'iang-kuo* of the legalists!), they must heed my words.[7] (Italics added.)

He then explains how local officials, after three years of probation and nine more years of able service, and having by then an adequate salary, knowledge of the local situation, and financial and administrative autonomy, would be linked so closely with the territory under their jurisdiction, almost with a feeling that they belonged to it, that they would do everything to further its interests and defend it. In this way poverty, red tape, and greedy clerks, the threefold plague of rural China, could be eliminated.

Ku T'ing-lin becomes even more eloquent in his disapproval of the silver tax. Contemporary observers could not understand the promise of progress contained in the vigorous strides of a market and money economy, and were quite indifferent to its somewhat doubtful advantages, seeing only the resulting havoc in the countryside. Where could the peasant in a remote rural district get the money for the tax from, and silver at that? In his essay on taxes—on purpose called *Ch'ien-liang lun*,[e15] because the then customary expression for taxes was composed of the two constituents of taxes in kind and money: grain and copper cash—he compares the plight of the countryman with that of someone who raises sheep and wants horses; and he declares that those who intend to make the country rich by piling up silver are like people offering wine to allay starvation.

There were other targets for vehement attack in late Ming society. The examination system, the field he knew best, was constantly under fire. In an essay on the stipendiary government students (*Sheng-yüan lun*),[e16] the number of whom he estimated to be close on 500,000, Ku pointed out that these candidates, trained to compose futile and formalistic examination papers following a set pattern— the notorious "eight-legged essays" (*pa-ku wen-chang*)— were lacking in any practical knowledge and completely useless for the administrative jobs for which they were intended.

As for the course of studies, his abomination was of course the Neo-Confucian *li-hsüeh* and the voluminous *yü-lu*, those countless collections of oracles, in which disciples had noted down the sayings, the *logia*, of their masters. He flatly asserted that these were nothing other than *ch'an-hsüeh*, shallow, intuitionist Dhyana-Buddhism (Zen). Blinded by his righteous wrath against Buddhism in general and the disintegrating influence of Mad Ch'an in particular, he even went so far as to declare that Li Cho-wu was "the worst among all the mean fellows who ever dared recklessly and unscrupulously to revolt against the Sage".[8 and c17]

This fierce indictment of the great heretic certainly does not enhance the figure of Ku T'ing-lin. It does, however, clearly show the manifold contradictions of the time and the insurmountable limitations of even the keenest spirits dedicated to the Confucianist tradition. And yet, it is this man who wrote about himself thus in a poem:

> Alas, my nature is difficult to tame
> Poor and old, still more unyielding.[9 and c18]

Equally unyielding and fierce was the third of the political thinkers I intend to speak of: the hermit of Hunan, Wang Ch'uan-shan (1619-92), also known by his original name, Wang Fu-chih—besides which he indulged in half a dozen other names. The family, originating from Kao-yu, Kiangsu, in the lower Yangtze delta, but since the times of Yung-lo established in central Hunan at Heng-yang, had a scholarly tradition. His father was a follower of Chu Hsi, his uncle a poet, his elder brother a prolific writer of commentaries to the classics. His life followed the same pattern as that already mentioned with reference to Huang Tsung-hsi and Ku Yen-wu, who were his seniors, the one by nine, and the other by eleven years. Like Huang Li-chou, Wang joined the Renewal Society at twenty-one. He passed his provincial graduate's examination (*chü-jen*) in Wu-ch'ang, but could not go to the examinations in Peking, for this was the year 1642, with Li Tzu-ch'eng advancing into Hunan and the other leader of the peasant rising, Chang Hsien-chung, threatening Hupei. The leaders of rebel bands, themselves uneducated, urgently required to have scholars around them, both to write proclamations, manifestos, etc., and to lend them prestige and authority. So Chang Hsien-chung, when he occupied Heng-yang the following year, tried to enlist young Wang. Wang succeeded in escaping enlistment by means of a self-inflicted wound, and took refuge in a hut on the Heng-shan mountain, significantly styled "Retreat of continuing dreams" (*Hsü-meng an*).[20] But the dreams did not continue. After the fall of Peking, Wang wrote a poem of 100 verses, entitled "Lament and indignation" (*Pei-fen shih*).[21] After the defeat of the pretender in Nanking, he wrote a second "Lament and indignation". Wang then made up his mind to join the resistance movement, but had a difference of opinion with the governor of Hunan. So, after the capture of the other Ming pretender in Fukien, there came a third "Lament and indignation". However, his hopes were re-aroused by the appearance of a new pretender, the Prince of Kuei (who later became a Christian). Wang joined his "court" in Kwangtung after having unsuccessfully defended his home-town against the Manchu invader. He was well received by the famous Christian minister of this prince, Ch'ü Shih-ssu, and stayed two years at the southern court, where, however, he soon made enemies by criticizing the factional struggles. He later wrote a chronicle of these events. Finally, in 1650—one year later than Huang Li-chou—Wang abandoned the hopeless Ming cause and retired from politics. (But when he learned about the flight of the Prince of Kuei to Burma in 1661, he wrote another "Lament and indignation".)

From now on he lived the life of a hermit among the inaccessible mountain fastnesses of Hunan, taking his final refuge at Mount Shih-ch'uan (from which his name derives). During this period, he wrote book after book, and married three times. There are only two incidents to report. Shortly before his death, the wandering monk Fang I-chih,[c22] another outstanding mind of the seventeenth century, visited him, but failed to win him over to Buddhism. Seven years later, in 1678, when Wu San-kuei, one of the three independent petty kings who seceded from the Manchus in southern China, proclaimed himself emperor in Wang's home-town, Wang declined to address memorials to him. This attitude was interpreted three years later, when the secession was over and the Manchu power definitively stabilized, as loyalty to the new dynasty. But the staunch Ming loyalist refused presents and official visits.

The rest consists of book titles. But I shall not burden you with a bibliography which is in any case an extraordinarily complex one. All I shall say is this: his works were not published during his lifetime—this being the reason for his relative obscurity until the nineteenth century, when the first edition of his collected works was published. The printing blocks of this edition were destroyed during the Taiping rebellion. A second edition, sponsored by Tseng Kuo-fan, contained 58 titles in 288 chapters. The so-called definitive edition of the *Ch'uan-shan i-shu*,[c23] consisting of 70 titles in 358 chapters, appeared in 1933 in Shanghai. (In Paris we do not have it.) Among these numerous titles, the most important are the philosophical works. But they frequently contain political comments, such as may be found in the "Meaning of the Shu-ching historically exemplified" (*Shang-shu yin-i*),[c24] or in the "Exoteric commentary to the Book of Changes" (*Chou-i wai-chuan*),[c25] or in the annotated commentaries on a treatise by the Sung philosopher Chang Tsai, whom he considered as his master. He also wrote books on Buddhism, and commentaries to Lao-tzu and to Chuang-tzu, considered as among the best. Finally there is a group of short political tracts, such as the "Yellow Book" (*Huang-shu*,[c26] 1656), and the "Nightmare" (*O-meng*,[c27] 1682), and his two best-known works, the *Tu T'ung-chien lun*[c28] (1687, 30 chapters) and the *Sung-lun*[o29] (15 chapters). These are collections of historico-political essays, also in the form of commentaries, the first on the historical work, *Tzu-chih t'ung-chien*, by Ssu-ma Kuang, and the second on the Sung History. Wang Ch'uan-shan died of asthma at 74 *sui*, ten years after Ku T'ing-lin and three before Huang Li-chou, with whom he had never had any direct contact. His epitaph, written by himself, reads as follows:

> Tomb of the last servant of the Ming, Wang Fu-chih.
> I have cherished a solitary loyalty like Liu Yüeh-shih (i.e. Liu K'un, 270-317, a patriot noted for his devotion to the Chin dynasty), yet (unlike him) have had no opportunity to offer my life. I have striven for the true doctrines of Chang Heng-ch'ü (i.e. Chang Tsai, 1020-77), yet my strength has not permitted me to attain to them. Fortunate though I am to return unmolested to this grassy mound, I feel saddened for all eternity (by my failure).[o30]

There are several reasons why it is extremely difficult to take Wang Ch'uan-shan's measure. In the first place, the claims made for him as a pioneer of nationalism, an exponent of materialism, and an early forerunner of Marxism were established very late, at the end of the nineteenth and the beginning of the twentieth century, by a generation in quest of a native pedigree. Secondly, his works, alarmingly numerous, were not printed until two centuries after his death, and were never properly edited, far less subjected to a systematic, scientific examination. Then again there is the most serious difficulty of a hermetic vocabulary and a frequently sibylline style full of allusions, baffling all attempts at translation.

I should like to illustrate this state of affairs with an example taken from his historical works, which are steeped in a peculiar kind of Neo-Confucian philosophy. Like his contemporaries, Wang Ch'uan-shan was an adversary of the intuitive mind (*hsin*) of Wang Yang-ming, but he maintained the formidable concept of *li*—the idea of an ingrained pattern of things, of an organic, reasonable law— as a fundamental metaphysical concept. However, according to Wang, apart from phenomena there is no Tao, and function alone determines the form of things. Now this concept, together with his evolutionary philosophy of nature, when transposed into the politico-historical field, led him to the discovery of something approaching "objective laws", which he frequently propounded in the course of his historical reflections. His basic concept of *shih*[o31]— which might be translated as power of prevailing conditions, tendency, trends—he defines as a force which must be followed and which cannot be opposed, i.e., *necessity*. Therefore, to obey necessary trends, to be in accordance with what ought to be, is reasonable.[10 and o32] There is, you must admit, a strangely Hegelian flavour about this. The resemblance is all the more remarkable because Wang Ch'uan-shan, who never himself challenged his Weltgeist by advocating revolution or radical reforms, has been, not unlike Hegel, adopted as prophet by radicals and revolutionary leaders. I shall come back to this point.

Let us now see how the objective laws of history, necessity and reason work according to Wang. At the outset of the *Tu T'ung-chien lun* we find the assertion that the evolution of China from feudalism to the prefectural system was a necessary development. Wang demolishes with gusto the Confucian legend of a golden age. In remote antiquity men were very near to barbarians and savage beasts. The chaos of that primitive age could not be changed by the legendary sage-kings before the times were ripe. Besides, if the popular Confucianist thesis about a golden age constantly deteriorating and becoming more and more decadent were correct, men must certainly by now have changed into demons. But on the contrary, the people of today in the empire of the prefectural system (*chün-hsien chih t'ien-hsia*,[o33] an expression constantly used by Wang) are much easier to govern than they used to be. The seeds of this system were in existence long before feudal kingdoms were doomed. Then, the times being ripe, the feudal kingdoms were abolished and the united empire of Ch'in arose. Thus, the two-thousand-year-old prefectural system cannot be changed. It was a necessary development, which could not have happened if it were contrary to reason. An eternal division between nobles and peasants is not justified by the heavenly, natural distribution of talents, which frequently goes contrary to these lines of cleavage. Therefore, it is again natural and necessary that a civil service and the examination system should have taken the place of the election of officials by recommendation. In general, "the post-Han empire is governed by post-Han laws", and every age has its own institutions peculiar to it. Nobody is able to turn the clock back, and the anachronistic application of the models of antiquity can only lead to anarchy and chaos.

I should like to quote here in full a passage on the inapplicability of ancient institutions to modern times, characteristic both of Wang's revolutionary iconoclasm and of his Taoistic fatalism:

> The ancient institutions were designed to govern the ancient world, and cannot be applied to the present day. Therefore the wise man does not try to set up detailed systems. One uses what is right for today to govern the world of today, but this does not mean that it will be right for a later day. Therefore the wise man does not try to hand down laws to posterity. Thus neither the "Book of History" nor Confucius describes feudalism, the well-field system, the triennial and sexennial meetings of feudal lords, the system for punitive expeditions, the establishment of offices or the awarding of benefices. How then should someone who is not the equal in virtue of the emperors Shun and Yü or Confucius still presume on the basis of his reading to lay down a system of laws for all time? ... Situations change, conditions are different. ... It is not necessary that one consult all the ages of the past and try to follow all their usages. In my writings I have sought the source of success and failure in government and tried to bring my ideas into accord with the fundamental principles of the governments of the sages. But when it comes to questions of particular facts and laws, then one must follow the times and try to determine what is fitting in each case. Every

age has its own tensions (rhythm); every affair has its contractions (contingent circumstances). It is better therefore to have no inflexible judgments, lest one should, by clinging to a single idea, do violence to the Tao. . . . One should not try to force the world to follow his own particular views.

The passage is taken from the famous *Hsü-lun*,[34] the four concluding essays of the *Tu T'ung-chien lun*, where Wang expounds his views on the writing of history. What we appreciate in history is that we may learn from the past how to master the future. If history records only a profusion of isolated facts without giving the main outlines of political action and without providing a model for studying the mechanics of former success and failure, then what is the use of history? According to Wang, history is a guide to practice, but not a collection of set rules, of fixed and unchanging formulas. This is the final word of the *Hsü-lun*.

But let us come back to the question of historical necessity, or, rather, let us see what this exponent of seventeenth-century ideas regarded as historical necessity. We have already heard his views about feudalism and the bureaucratic unified empire on the prefectural pattern. Institutions of a certain period form a coherent whole from which you cannot detach the parts and place them in a changed environment, because in the new context they would no longer work, no longer fulfil their function. The ancient system of local selection and recommendation of officials, for instance, cannot be restored. Similarly, equal distribution of land on the model of the well-field system is impossible today, although it was necessary under the primitive conditions of antiquity, when there were no proprietors, no regular taxes, and eighteen hundred tiny feudal countries, and when the royal power had to portion out land in order to bring waste land under cultivation and prevent large tracts of it remaining uncultivated. Later, however, when private property had developed naturally and automatically from the moment when Ch'in concentrated power and wealth in the hands of one ruler, and when force and intelligence had become, for both high and low, the only title to possession, the necessity for private landownership was firmly established. Egoism and inequality are the necessary marks of the *chün-hsien chih t'ien-hsia*. Therefore, land reforms cannot be carried out. For it is contrary to reason "to wish to wipe out force and intelligence in the whole empire and distribute land equally among the weak and the silly and still remain the only usurper, above all provinces. Even daily slaughter would only make the powerful more ferocious."[12] The Son of Heaven occupies his position not as the maintainer of the common weal, but thanks to the atomization of the humble. Humanity (*jen*) and justice (*i*) are merely fetters used by the ruler for keeping the empire under control. Under these circumstances landreform would be impracticable. Moreover, taxes are complex, officials are cruel, clerks are overbearing, so that when simple peasants receive land, it is not a blessing, but a calamity. The powerful landlords take away half the profit, and the peasants end up as agricultural slaves. There is only one way to alleviate their burden: lighter corvées, less taxes, and more restraint on the greediness of officials. Then people will not be afraid to possess land, big landlords will not be able to hoard it, and the latifundia will come to an end without any need for imposing a limitation on the size of estates. Land no more belongs to the emperor than does Heaven and Earth, and he cannot distribute it. He can keep the people under his control and use their manpower, but he cannot usurp rights to land, for the land belongs to the people, to everybody. Dynasties come and go, but the land remains the same.

It would be an understatement to say that Wang had no illusions. The view adopted by the new scientific generation in China is nearer to the truth—namely, that Wang took a more realistic, scientific stand than those who, in the manner of Huang Li-chou and Ku T'ing-lin, advocated reforms in order to check the concentration of power under absolutism. My own view is that Wang was first and foremost a conscious demolisher of Utopia, a tremendous overthrower of Confucian arguments and illusions. Secondly, he was also, though unconsciously, a defender of the interests of the new middle class, which he instinctively felt were better taken care of by an absolute monarchy than by a Confucian bureaucracy.

Typical of this mentality are Wang's ideas concerning necessity with reference to military matters, which afford another example of the working of the Chinese Weltgeist of the seventeenth century. One of the most cherished of the Confucianists' ideas was the militia system or peasant army, described by Wang as "lodging the troops in the peasantry" (*yü ping yü nung*).[c35] The peasant militia, he explains, is a feudal institution suitable for feudal times, when war was waged by lords who were near neighbours, and was a matter of Chinese against Chinese. But the development of military techniques since the Warring States period, and even more since the Han dynasty, when uprisings within the country and barbarian pressure from without the empire required professional military skill, today make a re-establishment of the militia system impossible. To restore it would only mean bad soldiers and uncultivated land, because soldiers of agricultural colonies (*t'un-t'ien*) are no soldiers, and peasants in uniform become accustomed to eating without working and turn robbers. The ideal of combining the civil and the military is irretrievably lost and cannot be restored, in the same way as the well-field system or corporal punishments cannot be set up again. Moreover, earning a living is one of man's inborn, natural capacities. It is better to let things alone (it is tempting to say "adopt the principles of *laisser-faire*") than to have a Welfare State.

As already mentioned, Wang Ch'uan-shan was hailed in modern times as the prophet of nationalism. It is in fact true that few Confucianists laid claim to China's national superiority, for although they were imbued with the notion of China's cultural superiority, to a degree at which it was certainly resented by non-Chinese neighbours as being a mark of arrogance, they still believed, at least theoretically, in the validity of the dictum of Confucius that within the four seas all men are brothers, and they had learnt from history, due to a succession of alien dynasties, that barbarians

could be civilized. The traditional yardstick still held good:
neither race nor nationality was the ultimate standard, but
civilization—in other words, the adoption of Chinese habits
and values. All the more striking, therefore, is Wang
Ch'uan-shan's attempt to provide scientific and historical
reasons for the prominence of China as a national state, on
the grounds that the Chinese were a distinct and different
race. No doubt the national resistance against the Manchu
invaders that had taken place in his lifetime had caused him
to give much thought to the problem of the co-existence of
Chinese and non-Chinese. So far as I know, he had never
been in the northern frontier provinces, but he had direct
experience of aborigines when living among the Miao and
Yao tribes of the Hunan mountains. It was shortly after his
time there, in 1656, that he wrote the "Yellow Book" (*Huang
-shu*), the first trumpet-call of nationalism. But the *Tu
T'ung-chien lun*, written thirty years later, is impregnated
with a nationalism no less virulent. Since no modern study
of the sources of Chinese nationalism has so far been made,
we do not know if foreign influences were at work in this
early period. I would tentatively suggest that it seems likely
that the national disaster at the end of the Ming dynasty,
along with Wang's evolutionary method of interpreting
history, together provide sufficient explanation of his exacer-
bated feelings of national pride and his original, if not quite
isolated or unique, rationalization of this feeling.

First let me quote two passages on the dissimilarity and
incompatibility of Chinese and barbarian ways:

> Barbarians and Chinese are born on different earth. The
> earth being different, climate is different, customs are
> different, and thus everything they know and do is
> different.[13]

> The strength of the barbarians lies in the rudimentary
> character of their laws and institutions. As long as
> their shelter, food, and clothing remain crude and bar-
> baric, as long as they continue to foster a violent and
> savage temper in their people and do not alter their
> customs, they may enjoy great advantage. And at the
> same time, because of this China may escape harm.

But if they once begin to change and adopt Chinese ways, then the advantages of their situation will also change. They may thereby in time grow braver and mightier than the Chinese, which will be an advantage gained, but they will also open the way for eventual weakness. Therefore it is said that, as fish forget each other in the rivers and lakes, so men should forget each other and follow their own ways and principles. While the barbarians are content to roam about in pursuit of water and pasture, practising archery and hunting, preserving no distinction between ruler and subject, possessing only rudimentary marriage and governmental systems, ranging back and forth over their territory in accordance with seasonal demands, then China can never control or rule them. And as long as the barbarians do not realize that *cities* can be fortified and maintained, that *markets* bring profit, that *fields* can be cultivated and *taxes* exacted, as long as they do not know the glory of elaborate *marriage* and *official systems*, then they will continue to look upon China as a perilous and inhospitable bed of thorns. In like manner the Chinese who are seized and carried off to the lands of the barbarians will regard them with hatred and bitterness and refuse to serve them. The two lands will ignore each other to the advantage of both. It is in accordance with the ordinances of Heaven and the dictates of human feeling that each should thus find delight only in his own ways.[14] (Italics added.)

This sounds very reasonable and is consistent with Chinese history. It is rather more sinister and also more symptomatic when Wang suggests, when discussing the wars of Emperor Han Wu-ti, that although they may have been harmful at the time, they should, from the point of view of national history, be regarded as highly beneficial deeds inspired by Heaven[15]; or when, speaking of conquests by guile and violence, he proclaims outright that faithfulness, righteousness, and other moral duties are good in intercourse between human beings, but are not appropriate to barbarians.[16 and c36] But again, Wang shows penetrating in-

sight in his comments on the change from chaos to culture
and back to chaos again, as exemplified by Northern China,
which, formerly the embodiment of Chinese civilization,
was now a backward borderland, and by south-eastern
China, which prior to Han times had been wholly barbarian, was still looked down upon in Sung times, but which
in his day had become the real cultural and economic centre
of the country.[17]

It is also rather frightening to hear the humanist Wang
Ch'uan-shan compare man to ants. He has been arguing
that, the instinct of self-preservation being the natural law
of all species from the tiniest insect to man, protection of
one's own kind (*pao-lei*)[o37] and security for the group (*wei-
ch'ün*)[o38] are therefore the essential functions of a political
organization. He goes on:

> Even the ants have leaders who rule their ant-hills, and if
> other insects come to attack their nests, the leader
> gathers the ants together and leads them against their
> enemies to destroy them and prevent further intru-
> sion. Thus he who would lead the ants must know the
> way to protect his group. Even so, if the ruler of the
> empire gives no thought to the future and does not
> consider well the importance of maintaining its fron-
> tiers, then he is unable to command respect or keep
> order within the empire. When danger threatens from
> outside, he has no means of warding it off; when natural
> disasters strike, he has no means of securing the people
> against them. He is unable to pass the succession on
> to his own posterity or to *protect his own kind*. (Italics
> added.) Thus, the kingly way comes to an end. This
> is what the *Spring and Autumn Annals* most deplored.

An earlier paragraph of this chapter runs:

> Therefore he who is wise enough to make little of him-
> self yet strong enough to govern the empire and *pro-
> tect his own kind* becomes the chief, and he who pro-
> vides *security for his group* becomes its ruler. (Italics
> added.) . . . There might be abdications, successions,
> and even changes of mandate (i.e. revolutions), yet
> never should a foreign dynasty (lit. an alien kind) be

permitted to interrupt the succession [of Chinese sovereigns].[18]

Preservation and continuity are of primary importance to the nation, and all institutions, ceremonies, and regulations merely secondary. And in the postface of the *Huang-shu*, Wang Ch'uan-shan declares (an unheard-of heresy in Confucian China!) that "If the race (*tsu-lei*) cannot be firmly established, what is the use of all the phrases about humanity and justice?"[c39]—i.e., the cardinal virtues of Confucianism. In one sentence we have here the Taoist sage turned nationalist tribune.

For nations which have long since recovered from the ailments of infancy the first stammerings of nationalism are less attractive than they are for peoples who are fighting for national sovereignty. We should certainly not commit the error of belittling the achievement of Wang Ch'uan-shan. On the other hand, there is no need to err in the other direction and regard those nations which were oppressed during the nineteenth century as exceptional, saintly organisms congenitally incapable of oppressing other nations either in the past or in the future.

Anyway, at the beginning of the First World War, about 1915, a Society for the study of Wang's writings (*Ch'uan-shan hsüeh-she*)[c40] was established in Ch'ang-sha, and up until the early 'thirties it regularly published a periodical called *Ch'uan-shan hsüeh-pao*. This club, founded to study and perpetuate the teachings of the great Hunan master, was one of the numerous learned societies for students to which the students who were soon to be engaged in the May Fourth Movement of 1919 belonged. Needless to say, among the active members of this club we find another Hunanese, more famous than Wang Ch'uan-shan—Chairman Mao Tse-tung.

And this brings us to the conclusion of my first two lectures. It is evident that there is need for serious study of each of the three men discussed, especially the last one. Research of this kind will certainly be fostered in China, but it is doubtful whether, in the present circumstances, the Chinese will be able to assess anew the value of the giants of the seventeenth century. For obvious reasons. After my very

AS—4

superficial outline of the tenets of Huang Li-chou, Ku T'ing-lin, and Wang Ch'uan-shan, it might be possible to link the thought of the first with *democracy*, of the second with *science*, and of the third with *nationalism*—that is to say, with the driving forces of the New China of the twentieth century. But this is only justifiable as a short-cut, a convenient means of showing the link between early and late forms of the same social strata and the development and metamorphosis of a few fundamental ideas that have been active during a particular stage of development of our modern society. But all such generalizations and ruminations on commonplaces should no longer be a part of the kind of research that ought to be undertaken today.

In order to assess these three men at their true value and establish the importance of their work and the consequences it bore, it will be necessary to acquire a thorough knowledge of the lesser figures, their schools, connections, surroundings, and all the infinitely diverse and complex life of the seventeenth century in China. Since very little has so far been done in this field, and since, as I have tried to show again and again, it is full of contradictions, there is an enormous task in store for the younger generation. If I have succeeded in suggesting that this task is not only arduous but also rewarding, then I shall be happy to feel that my labours have not been in vain.

Fontenay-aux-Rose, 28 December 1962 to 5 January 1963

III

A HANDBOOK OF LOCAL ADMINISTRATIVE PRACTICE OF 1793

Today, with a change of subject, we have to make a great leap forward—in time, that is; for the exact date of the handbook of local administrative practice I am going to talk about is 1793.

In a country which can justifiably be described as bureaucratic, there had quite naturally always been a great deal of interest in problems of administration. The civil service being almost the only outlet for the ruling class of scholar officials, and writers of books being almost solely recruited from among the literati, it is only to be expected that from a very early date books were written laying down the principles of administrative practice, full of advice and warnings to civil servants, and of moral dissertations on what a local official should and should not do. A distinction must be made between this type of literature and the large class described by the bibliographers as "government books" (*cheng-shu*),[1] comprising vast encyclopaedias and collections of administrative documents such as the *T'ung-tien*, the *T'ung-chih*, the *T'ung-k'ao*, and the various *Hui-yao*. The bibliographers somewhat illogically established another class, the *chih-kuan*,[2] which was divided into two sub-classes, the first consisting of books on official institutions (*kuan-chih*),[3] such as the *Han-kuan* or the *T'ang liu-tien* or the *Li-tai chih-kuan piao*, and the second, under the misleading label *kuan-chen*[4] (exhortations, admonitions), consisting in fact of all the practical guides. These guides had a great vogue in the eighteenth and nineteenth centuries, but only two or three Sung specimens have survived. Able governors or prefects either re-edited earlier works or wrote new ones, for which they usually found attractive titles suitable for handbooks, such as "Compass" (*chih-nan*), "Outlines" (*yao-lüeh* or *chü-yao*), "Essentials" (*hsü-chih*), or "Made easy" ("Easy to read", *pien-lan*).[5]

We know that these guides were eagerly studied by officialdom in the past. But it is pertinent to ask whether old handbooks, written for their colleagues by a vanished class in a form of society which has long ago ceased to exist, can have any interest for us today? The answer to this question is an emphatic Yes! They are of interest mainly for two reasons. First, because of a general interest in bureaucratic societies in our time, and second because of an interest in China in particular as providing an historical example of a great and highly developed bureaucratic society.

Recently three studies on this last topic have been published, which are perhaps the most revealing books on China ever written, though difficult to read. They are Ho Ping-ti's *Studies on the population of China 1369-1953*,[1] Hsiao Kung-ch'üan's *Rural China. Imperial control in the nineteenth century*,[2] and Ch'ü T'ung-tsu's *Local Government in China under the Ch'ing*.[3] My point in mentioning these books, written by three Chinese scholars and published within a short time of each other in the United States, is not so much to illustrate that a demand exists for this type of research, as to indicate how rewarding the study of official hand-books, if intelligently done, can be, for it is precisely the guides to administrative practice that have been one of the main sources of the three books mentioned—especially, of course, the last.

The problems I am concerned with here, however, go far beyond the official sphere, for there is much more sub-stantial food for thought to be culled from the administra-tive guides than a casual glance might lead us to believe. This remark is not intended as a stricture on what has already been done, but rather as a justification for my long-sustained interest in the subject and my painstaking attempt to translate a particularly crabbed text, of which you shall soon have a few examples.

The text is the *Hsüeh-chih i-shuo*[6] ("Opinions on appren-ticeship in government") by Wang Hui-tsu.[7] Wang Hui-tsu came from a Chekiang town south-east of Hangchow. Being poor, he chose to become a private secretary to local officials, and served in this capacity under sixteen different prefects over a period of more than thirty years, in Kiangsu and Chekiang. The post of private secretary—an essential cog in the machinery of local administration—was well paid in those days, especially in the case of private secretaries con-cerned with judicial matters, which was the case with Wang. He became so highly specialized and acquired so much ex-perience in this field that he had no time left for climbing higher up the hierarchy, and only reached the next step, that of acting magistrate, before retiring to his home dist-rict. He was known in his time as a very competent official, and in addition he succeeded in compiling the first Index to the twenty-four Dynastic Histories (the famous *Shih-*

hsing yün-pien,[08] which was still in use in my student days). It might also be added that he was a good friend of the historians Shao Chin-han and Chang Hsüeh-ch'eng. But with his two works on local government he acquired national celebrity.

The first of these was a guide for private secretaries called "Precepts for Administrative Practice" (*Tso-chih yao-yen*),[09] soon followed by a "Supplement" (*Hsü Tso-chih yao-yen*),[09] both published in 1785-86, the first consisting of 40, the second of 26 short notices. Some of these have been translated by Mrs. Sybille van der Sprenkel in her recent book on "Legal Institutions in Manchu China".[4] It was probably the success of the *Tso-chih yao-yen* that led Wang Hui-tsu to write a second guide, this time for magistrates. This is the *Hsüeh-chih i-shuo* (1793) and its two supplements, the *Hsüeh-chih hsü-shuo* ("More on apprenticeship in government", 1794), and the *Hsüeh-chih shuo-chui*[010] ("Appendix to apprenticeship in government", 1800). These three booklets consist, like the earlier ones, of rather short articles, and contain respectively 124, 50 and 14 paragraphs.

All that need be added about Wang Hui-tsu's personal biography is that he took his degree of provincial graduate (*chü-jen*) after failing *eight times*, and his metropolitan graduate's degree (*chin-shih*) at the age of forty-six, after failing *three times*. He became paralysed in 1795 and began then to write his autobiography, which he continued until his last hour. There remains, however, much to say about Wang Hui-tsu the official, representing as he did the perfect type of eighteenth-century Chinese bureaucrat—of the honest kind—with all his excellent qualities and human shortcomings, kindly wisdom and appalling limitations and shortsightedness.

All this comes out strikingly in his works, the priceless value of which lies in the natural, confident, taking things for granted, self-satisfied tone of *an official speaking to officials, a bureaucrat to other bureaucrats, a scholar to his equals*. There is an atmosphere of members of the same social set talking confidentially among friends—a "between ourselves" touch; and the we-group is never disturbed by the they-group, the people, who play the role of eternally anonymous subjects, like the "invisible" sceneshifters in the Kabuki theatre who are disguised in black clothes. For this reason, Wang Hui-tsu's book has a more authentic ring than the best of sociological analyses could have, and is more concrete, more direct, and more meaty.

So without further ado I shall go straight to the heart of the matter and begin with the central figure of local administration, the magistrate. The heads of departments (*chou*) and districts (*hsien*),[c11] usually referred to as *fu-mu kuan*[c12]—an expression unquestionably referring more to the submissiveness to the magistrate's authority on the part of the people under his jurisdiction than to the parental care he lavished on them—represented, and acted for, the central government, and were almighty as the executive authorities throughout the country. Almighty, however, with certain qualifications, because not only did the magistrate have to reckon with his immediate superiors, the higher provincial officials, but even more because at every step, as we shall see, he was dependent upon, if not at the mercy of, his numerous subordinates and underlings. Nevertheless, he had to assume responsibility for everything in the huge area he presided over—for maintaining law and order, collecting taxes, giving decisions in most of the legal cases that arose, and for the general administration of the salt monopoly, granaries, communications, postal service, police, education, and so on and so forth. In short, if he had possessed the qualifications for carrying out all his duties, he would have been a genius. Instead, he was an all-round blunderer, a harassed Jack-of-all-trades, an easy-going member of the mediocracy, eternally worried as to how to steer clear of Scylla and Charybdis—the people below and the authorities above. Most important of all, he had to be on friendly terms with the very influential local gentry—the intelligentsia and the only literate men in the territory he was in charge of.

Let me illustrate this with some quotations from and references to the "Apprenticeship in Government":

Local authorities are in charge of paying respects to

literate men and caring for the people, they have to welcome and escort visitors, visit superiors, and entertain colleagues. Every day there is a lot of public business to transact, and the intricacy of accounts and documents is appalling. Even a capable man has to rely on a private secretary, especially in view of differences in provincial rules and diversity of habits and customs, only known by those who are acquainted with the locality. (Paragraph 5.)

To be magistrate of a department or a district means to be in charge of a territory of 100 *li*. Now it takes at least twelve months to gain even a general impression of people's sentiments and of the habits and customs inside these hundred miles. Again it takes another twelve months before it is possible to act in accordance with the sentiments of the people and with their material interests, for it is not possible to do anything until their confidence has been won. Only after a thorough understanding of all kinds of affairs can there be established a bond of co-operation between the magistrate and the intelligentsia and the people. Merit ratings and inspection of accounts occur every three years, so there is no question of rapid success. Those who are in a hurry to push themselves forward, who hope to be transferred after a short time to a higher post, who run after lucrative positions before they get warmed up in their present post, do not care in the least about the people, and are indifferent to their joy and sorrow. . . . Why are magistrates called father-and-mother officials? Alas, nobody obliged them to become a magistrate. How can they fail to take the well-being of the people into account? (Paragraph 29.)

Wang Hui-tsu comments that it is much easier for a magistrate to carry out his duties in an out-of-the-way place than in a busy centre of communications. In the first case, he has few guests to entertain, few visitors to see off, his work is not constantly interrupted, and he can devote his twelve working hours entirely to the study of his files. Documents pouring in are immediately dispatched, business settled from day to day. Being in close contact with the people under his jurisdiction, it is easy to prevent corrupt practices among servants and clerks, to win people's confidence, and ultimately to gain a reputation. In a busy place, on the contrary, only two to four hours can be spared for official duties, and yet the magistrate's nerves are rapidly worn out. (30)

But remote regions and out-of-the-way posts also have their disadvantages. There is the language difficulty. Local dialects are difficult to understand at first, and if you use clerks and servants as interpreters you may never get the exact meaning of what people are saying. Wang Hui-tsu gives a piece of practical advice: take a native boy of eleven or twelve years of age and try to get acquainted with the local language by questioning him all day long. (35) Incidentally, he also recommends using simple and comprehensible language in all written public notices, since people usually find it difficult to understand the written language and soon tire trying to read long-winded and verbose documents. It is best to use rhymed phrases, for instance eight sentences of four words each or six sentences of five to six words each, the characters being copied in nice calligraphy easy to read. (57)

There are other difficulties, a major one being how to get inside information. Let us hear what Wang Hui-tsu has to say on this point:

Human attitudes, habits, and customs are different in every place. . . . When you arrive at a new post, you must not make hasty decisions. For if decisions are not in agreement with local public opinion, discussions arise; and if you persist in attempting to carry them out, the use of force will be difficult. At every audience, you should let a few old and experienced men among the crowd in the court come up before you and you should ask them questions about customs and habits. Thus judgments will be fair, and the law will be in a natural harmony with human feelings. If in one day you understand one thing, in a hundred days you can understand a hundred things, and after a few months all things will be clear. Not only will official business be conducted successfully, but orders will pass along as smoothly as flowing water. (36)

In order to acquire a knowledge of the locality, you need informants, giving preference to the gentry. Here is how Wang Hui-tsu proceeded:

When I arrived in Ning-yüan (a district in south-west Hunan where he was magistrate for four years) I was like an ignoramus. So whenever guests arrived I humbly questioned each of them about local conditions and asked for the names of rowdies and ruffians (*kun-fei*,[13] the village bullies). Secretly I prepared a small notebook in which I carefully noted everything my guests told me as soon as they departed. Concerning pettifoggers, bullies, and thieves, I put on record age, features, and abode. Every time before going into the court hall I glanced through my notebook, and if I saw people bearing a resemblance to those recorded in it, I picked them out and gave my instructions. Everybody was dumbfounded. Thus the law was enforced without offence and before the end of the year I knew the essential facts about the territory under my jurisdiction. ... If later on my capacities were over-estimated, it was simply due to this little trick of mine. (37)

Of course, the magistrate must never disclose the names of his informants, for they might easily become the victims of revenge. As Wang Hui-tsu puts it: "To make trouble for them on account of their contribution to the maintenance of order would be impossible as far as right conduct (*i*) is concerned and one's conscience would certainly not be at ease." (38)

How should the magistrate behave towards his superiors? To steer a middle course between obligations and personal relationships is a ticklish problem:

It is the duty of an official to serve his superiors. An official task assigned by one's superior must not be refused, regardless of the hardships and difficulties involved. But when one's superior commands one to do him a personal favor, one must stay away from him.

One must act this way not only with regard to obviously personal matters, but even when personal intentions are merely implied in an official assignment, since any catering to such intentions will cause one to act against one's conscience . . . leading eventually to corruption of the law. One must sincerely make this understood when one's abilities first become appreciated by one's superior, by expressing a complete devotion to public duty to the exclusion of any private dealing. Should the superior take this as an inability to appreciate expediency, one should resign to preserve one's own character. (21)[5]

This was, of course, a Platonic recommendation, as can be seen from the following paragraphs:

When (a subordinate) official receives favored consideration from his superior, he indeed has gained an opportunity to realize his ambitions. But those already in a favored position will fear him; those about to receive favors will be jealous of him; those who fail to obtain favors will watch for an opportunity to push him out. A secret may leak out; rumors will follow. Superiors vary in their feelings about their subordinates. Even should all my present superiors like me, there is no certainty that my later superiors will feel the same way. Lo T'ung said: "The deeper the dislike, the craftier the slander." The man who receives favors walks in fear and trembling; those who have had the experience will know what I mean. (19)[6]

How can one avoid having displeased superior officials who try to pick faults? My answer is: in order to avoid this one has to be extra careful day in day out. A subordinate official can at any moment be involved in many public and private offences. Therefore those who assume office are called "those who will be found guilty" (*tai-tsui*).[c14] The only really guilty people are those who are greedy, cruel, or responsible for a deficit in the public funds. Other offences are simply public errors. It is better to resign office and keep the law than cling to the feeding trough and incur punishment. (22)

There were other dangers lurking, not the least of which was the employment of relatives. Wang Hui-tsu gives a stern warning against the appointment of sons, sons-in-law, and brothers-in-law to official positions:

> Those who have prestige acquire power. Those who have power acquire even more prestige. If you entrust (these three types of relative) with the correspondence, they will sell documents and traffic in warrants. If you commit legal cases to their care, they will negotiate for bribes and alter right and wrong. If you let them supervise granaries, they will be careless about deliveries and increase payments, engaging everywhere in corruption. It is difficult to count up all the evil practices. ... If their management is not catastrophic, the matter will not come to your ears, and then when it does, it is too late to take action. (?)
>
> Follow the law and you will destroy personal affection; follow personal affection and you will abuse the law. The problem is the same with all three [types of relatives], but it is worst with a son. Nothing need be said about the son who sacrifices the father for his own interests. But even the son who meticulously works for his father's benefit out of filial affection will inevitably subvert the father's proper performance of his duty. (85) Punish a son-in-law and you will alienate your daughter; punish a brother-in-law and you will alienate your wife. Should the official sacrifice affection and dismiss his relatives, he has already suffered much from the complication. It is better to choose aides (private secretaries) from among friends. The relationship between the official and his aides is based on duty. He treats them with respect only as long as they are loyal to their duties. If they are disloyal to their duties, there is nothing wrong in severing the relationship, or even punishing them by law. (86)[7]

On the other hand, a magistrate should treat his relatives with generosity in order not to deserve blame in his home district, but he must not go too far. After all, the official who sacrifices part of his salary in order to provide his relatives with food and clothing has nothing to reproach himself with. "If the heart is overflowing but resources are insufficient there is nothing to be done about it" is Wang's dry comment. (87)

As a general rule, it is better to support relatives financially than to entrust them with official duties. Supervising the granary and the treasury are the only jobs that can be assigned to a relative, and then only if he is an absolutely trustworthy person. (89) Usually, however, it is only good-for-nothing persons who follow an official from one post to another. "People employed in a magistrate's office generally go there looking for influence or profit. They are a *cloud of crows* which one of these days will leave the office and disperse in all directions." (90)

Elsewhere, Wang recommends that the magistrate should not take his young relatives with him to his post, the yamen being the worst place in the world for the education of young people. Gambling, obsequious servants, dissolute songs, the bad society of depraved actors and catamites are a constant temptation, not to speak of the weakening influence of rich food and fine clothes. (88) And then again he admits that a magistrate without a family is in an absolutely hopeless position. The keys always dangle at his side, and he cannot go out without taking the official seal with him. Concubines cannot be trusted, coming as they do from low families—at best, two or three out of a hundred are nice-looking and intelligent. What is worse, favourites soon take hold of authority and power.

Spied upon by hundreds of people around him, the magistrate must be very careful for his reputation. He should not drink, except in the evening behind closed doors. (93) He should, of course, enjoy music and women, but he must use self-restraint. He should not even indulge with exaggeration in the pleasures of poetry and painting, because if he looks impatient or annoyed when interrupted in his pastimes by official business, this may be the beginning of misfortune. And Wang Hui-tsu exclaims in a very eighteenth-century manner: "To be sure, human beings are not saints (*sheng-hsien*),[e15] and nobody is without passions. But you must be strict and restrain yourself. You can take a personal interest in things, but you should not let yourself be ensnared by things. In this way you will obtain them." (92)

A magistrate must stand alone in shouldering responsibilities. "If I do not have my own fixed opinions, but listen to what other people propose, then relatives will be the magistrate when I employ relatives, friends will be the magistrate when I employ friends, and when I employ servants, clerks, and runners, it will be servants, clerks and runners who will act as magistrate. If everyone possesses power and everyone becomes an official, the tail necessarily gets too big to be wagged, and the magistrate will be like a puppet." (63)

Let us leave the yamen now for the time being and follow the magistrate in the pursuit of his duties. There occur, for instance, the infrequent but serious cases of murder. "The weather may be hot or cold, the place may be near or far, but after the examination (of the defendant) one must immediately go out in order to prevent the culprit's witnesses entering the town to consult some petifogger (*sung-shih*).[16] If the culprit arrives half-way, then one has to choose a halting place and begin the questioning on the spot. The culprit not being prepared for the interrogation, it will be easy to get the facts." (77)

Wang Hui-tsu seems to have had a good deal of unpleasant experience with pettifoggers, for he deals several times with the subject, stressing the advantage of questioning defendants before they get instructions from petition-writers. In one of these paragraphs, he lets slip the following revealing remark: "Besides, when country people see high officials for the first time, they feel afraid of them." (76)

Then there are inquests. The magistrate should attend the post-mortem examination in person, touch the corpse with his own hands, inspect the wounds, scrutinize the stage of decay without shrinking from the fetid smell in summer, because you can never be sure whether coroners are cheating. (78)

There are also many cases which demand the making of exact measurements: quarrels over land, disputes about hilly land and field boundaries, litigation over canals and irrigation, cases of geomancy, etc. Swindle, trickery, humbug, and lies can only be prevented by meticulous and exact measuring and marking off of borders, boundaries, and limits, in the presence of the magistrate. (54)

Then there are thieves and robbers and their inseparable partners in fraud, the constables. Clever thieves usually furnish government runners with supplies, with a view to accusing them as accomplices if necessary. Wang Hui-tsu tells us that most magistrates pay no attention to such things, which makes it even worse for those who honestly try to do something about them. He recommends a device—although himself doubtful of its efficiency—which consists of keeping an eye on the constable and encouraging him to redeem his shortcomings by capturing thieves and robbers. (71)

An amazing chapter, called by the author "a contribution to the art of expelling beggars", deals with the serious problem of vagabondage created by natural calamities. In an age when the transfer of the grain reserve of one district to another for purposes of relief was expressly forbidden, country people flocked to the nearest district where there were grain reserves in the hope of escaping starvation. Wang Hui-tsu first reports the ingenious method invented by a former prefect for getting rid of an unruly crowd of boisterous beggars, which consisted in listing the beggars by name one by one, promising them money for the return journey, escorting them to the town, and arranging with the constables there to chase them away. This was a method, however, which did not always work. Wang once had to deal with a flood of beggars—the whole population of a neighbouring department which had been stricken by a bad harvest. These beggars inundated the thirty-six villages of the Hunan district under his jurisdiction. What did he do? He made every village mutually and collectively responsible for capturing and driving out the unfortunate beggars. And that was that. (73) Needless to say, they went to a neighbouring district.

I should like to round off the picture by describing Wang Hui-tsu's attitude towards religious and judicial matters—an attitude which was certainly shared by his colleagues and readers.

There are only three articles on religion, but they are very revealing, and I would strongly recommend all those who write about Confucianism as a religion to read them.

The first deals with the importance of the tutelary deity of the district town. "You should revere without exception all the gods of the ancestral temples and sanctuaries of the dynasty, but the tutelary god of the city *(ch'eng-huang shen)*[o17] has its particular importance as patron saint of the territory." He illustrates this point with the story of a repentant murderer "in order to show the usefulness of the city gods for official administrative purposes". (64)

Wang Hui-tsu distinguished between regional gods *(ti-fang t'u-shen)*[o18] and the local gods of the villages *(ko-hsiang t'u-ti-shen)*.[o19] About the former we read:

> Not only the city god should be revered but all the regional gods who are the subject of veneration and faith of the entire territory under jurisdiction. They must have meritorious virtues in the eyes of the people, since they get unceasing offerings. On account of their not being included in the statutory sacrifices, some people reject them. This cannot be allowed. Indeed, the majority of simple men and women do not fear the law of officials, but do fear the punishment of the gods. *Gods are not supernatural themselves, but they act supernaturally on the minds of those who believe in them.* Why then, what is the harm if local authorities enlarge upon and adapt this fear of the gods in order that people should become better and reform? Is this not the meaning of the Divine Way and of the established moral doctrine? (65)

And *we* may ask: is this not a perfect statement of the rationalistic and positivistic agnosticism of the eighteenth century?

It was customary, when praying for rain, for the people of Hunan to bring their local gods in procession to the yamen of the district town and to ask the officials to bow before them. This happened at Ning-yüan in the spring of

1789. About twenty images of village gods were brought, and permission was requested to bring them into the great hall of audience. Wang Hui-tsu flatly refused to perform the rite and made the following speech:

> You are making this procession on account of the urgent need of the people for rain. If the people need rain and the officials are unaware of it, the officials must be urged to take action by having the gods presented to them. Now, your present magistrate made his prayers before the people made them. So what is the meaning of all this? Moreover, when officials perform the rites, they make nine prosternations or six prosternations or three prosternations according to the fixed prescriptions of the State (*kuo*: the dynasty), without daring to add or to subtract. . . . Local gods of every village have a status equal to that of the local constable (*ti-pao*).[c20] The local magistrate cannot be treated on a par with the local constables. How then is it possible to treat the local gods as equals of the local magistrate, without regard to ceremonial and etiquette? You cannot run counter to ceremonial and etiquette and bring the gods before the magistrate. This would mean being too familiar with the gods. Besides, if your gods are intelligent, you should go and implore the city god, and you will then have no time to enter the city gate. If they are not intelligent, then they are but earthen idols. The Rites do not allow for the magistrate to bow and pray. It is not that I do not love the people, but it is impossible to act contrary to the canon of the Rites or to offend against the statutes of the State. So return home quickly with your gods! If you meet relatives and friends on your way, tell them of my words, and do not try to enter the city again. (66)

Since any commentary on this is superfluous, let us shift the scene and move to judicial matters. As former private secretary specializing in the law, Wang Hui-tsu has, of course, a lot to say about this subject. I shall, however, only pick out a few points that seem to me important. Needless to say, his thought is determined by the Confucianist legal doctrine of a balance between abstract law (*fa* or *li*),[c21] and human feelings, circumstances, imponderables (*ch'ing*).[c22] Here is an example of this spirit:

> Cases that turn on no absolute distinction between right and wrong and that can be reconciled are best settled with the help of relatives and friends. Adjudication is based on law, but reconciliation is based on the situation. Law must distinguish between right and wrong, but the situation may allow moderation of the strict standard of right and wrong. The right party's position will be endorsed by relatives and friends, and the wrong party will avoid punishment by the court. (49)[8]

This doctrine implies, however, that the law should, in all its harshness and severity, be applied whenever necessary, and that criminals with evil intentions should be pounced upon immediately and treated without mercy. Wang lays much stress on the need for close psychological observation of prisoners, and tells us that, although short-sighted, he always studied the faces of the accused, and recognized the guilty by their changes in colour, speech, etc. (43) He recommends placidity, and does not believe in the efficiency of the procedures of those brutish and blunt judges who intimidate the accused in an off-hand manner, slapping their faces a hundred times for the slightest reason, and applying all the accessories of legal procedure—cangue, manacles, and fetters—simultaneously. (44) It is certainly the case, and greatly to his credit, that Wang advocated that proceedings should be as humane as was compatible with Chinese law, and stressed reliance upon material proof and upon the evidence of witnesses as being far more trust-worthy than torture for extorting a confession of guilt. It was, however, only illegal torture which he rejected, a moving description of which is given in his *Hsüeh-chih i-shuo*, which incidentally is corroborated by a more detailed description provided, a hundred years later, by John Henry Gray, Archdeacon of Hong Kong. Let us first hear Wang:

> There exists a torture called "kneeling on a chain". Chains are laid on the ground and the culprit is made to kneel on them with his body bared. When this does

not suffice, a bar of wood is passed across the bend of his knees and pressed down at each end by two men. This torture is called "treading the bar" or "pressing the bar". It is an unbearable spectacle, particularly the terrible cries of agonizing pain. Twenty years ago (i.e. *c.* 1773) an (otherwise) capable official used this method in questioning a wily thief. Soon afterwards, he applied the same method to others than crafty thieves, later again to people accused of murder, and finally he used it in simple trials of civil conflicts and disputes. . . . The magistrate sits high at a table in the great hall; he can drink tea, he can smoke, he can eat and be comfortable. The culprit, kneeling at the other end of the hall, is starving and worn out, trembling with fear. Even if he should be an utterly depraved rascal, he will make mistakes in speaking. Listening placidly and severely scrutinizing his errors, handling him with flexibility, the magistrate will get all the information he requires. Nobody who loves the people will extort evidence by torture. (47)

And here is the testimony of John Henry Gray, published in London by Macmillan in 1878, in a book entitled *China. A History of the Laws, Manners, and Customs of the People*[9]:

Trials in Chinese courts of law are conducted by torture. . . . The judge when conducting a trial sits behind a large table, which is covered with red cloth. The prisoner is made to kneel in front of the table as a mark of respect to the court, by whom he is regarded as guilty until he is proved to be innocent. . . . As it is a rare thing for Chinese prisoners—mercy being conspicuously absent in the character of their judges—to plead guilty, trials are very numerous. During the course of the trial the prisoner is asked a great many leading questions which have a tendency to criminate him. Should his answers be evasive, torture is at once resorted to as the only remaining expedient.

Let me describe a few of the simplest modes of torture. The upper portion of the body of the culprit having been uncovered, each of his arms—he being in a kneeling posture—is held tightly by a turnkey, while a third beats him most unmercifully between the shoulders with a double cane. Should he continue to give evasive answers, his jaws are beaten with an instrument made of two thick pieces of leather, sewn together at one end. . . . The force with which this instrument of torture is applied to the jaws of the accused is in some instances so great as to loosen his teeth, and cause his mouth to swell to such a degree as to deprive him for some time of the powers of mastication. Should he continue to maintain his innocence, a turnkey beats his ankles by means of a hard piece of wood. . . . Should the prisoner still persist in declaring his innocence, a severer mode of torture is practised. This may be regarded as a species of rack. (A description follows.) When the prisoner has been thus bound, the questions are again put to him, and should his answers be deemed unsatisfactory, the double cane is applied with great severity to his thighs, which have previously been uncovered. I have known prisoners remain in this position for a considerable time, and the quivering motion of the whole frame, the piteous moans, and the saliva oozing from the mouth, afforded the most incontestible evidence of the extremity of the torture. Upon being released from the rack, they are utterly unable to stand. They are therefore placed in baskets and borne by coolies from the court of justice, falsely so-called, to the house of detention on remand. In the course of a few days they are once more dragged out to undergo another examination. Even this torture occasionally fails in extorting a confession of guilt. In all such cases another still crueller torture is enforced. The prisoner is made to kneel under a bar of wood, six English feet in length, and is supported by two upright pillars or posts of the same material. When the back of his neck has been placed immediately under it, his arms are extended along the bar, and made fast by cords. In the hollow of the back of his knee joints is laid a second

bar of equal dimensions, and upon this two men place
themselves, one at each end, pressing it down by their
weight upon the joints of the prisoner's knees, between
which and the ground chains are sometimes passed to
render the agony less endurable. . . . I have twice wit-
nessed this mode of torturing a culprit, and its severity
on both occasions was painfully evident.

I apologize for this painfully long quotation, but I think
it supplies the necessary background for understanding the
limitations of Wang Hui-tsu's liberalism. Indeed, I must
repeat that it was only *illegal* torture he protested against.

I am eager to leave the subject of torture, but I am
obliged to dwell on the question of illegality. This is a
pivotal question. What is legal and what illegal, and where
is the borderline, if any, between the two? To say the least
of it, the frontier-line seems to be floating, mobile, constantly changing, entirely unfixed. This fact is of the
greatest importance as soon as we begin to study the main
feature of Wang Hui-tsu's society: *corruption*. At the beginning of his book, he makes a generalized understatement
about corruption, when speaking about the private secretaries in charge of law and taxation, who were the main
aides of the magistrate:

Alas! It is difficult to speak about the principles of the
private secretary's profession. Formerly, when I was
twenty-two or twenty-three (i.e. 1752 or 1753) and was
first studying to be a private secretary, those who took
positions as judicial aides or tax accountants conducted
themselves with dignity as would a guest or a teacher
in another's house. From dawn till dusk they would
stay at their tables handling documents, not amusing
themselves with dice and chess or wasting money
drinking with one another. Whenever there was some
public business, they would cite the law and talk the
matter over, and if some higher official disagreed with
them they would have the courage to defend their
opinions. Their superiors treated them respectfully,
and followed their advice with trust. If they were
treated disrespectfully or had any of their advice re-

jected by their superiors, they would resign. If there chanced to be one or two who lacked self-respect, all the others would point them out in ridicule; there were never any flatterers. When I reached the age of thirty-seven or thirty-eight (i.e. 1767-68) it was still like this; but shortly thereafter, people became slightly more flexible and compromising. A few years later, a man who remained personally upright was regarded as unrealistic and impractical. It is difficult to swim against the current. Finally it became so bad that they made a trade of their influence and business was arranged by bribery, and men formed cliques and alliances to protect one another. *Not even two or three out of ten behaved uprightly.* New men entering this profession would usually pick up these evil ways from their mentors and would not know any better. (6)[10] (Italics added.)

Now, among the generally underpaid staff of the magistrate's office, it was the private secretaries who got the highest salary. Magistrates received a meagre nominal salary and a supplementary salary, significantly called "money to nourish honesty" (*yang-lien yin*),[c23] which was just enough to nourish the private secretaries, but far from enough to nourish honesty. How could it have been otherwise? The most a magistrate got varied between 500 and 1,000 taels per annum, while the annual expenses entailed by his post were ten times as much, not including personal expenses and salaries for secretaries and servants. The magistrate had, indeed, to meet very heavy expenses in making up the amounts of assigned contributions to government expenditure and accumulated deficits in the administration of granaries and treasuries. He also had to entertain superior officials passing through his area, and last, but not least, he had to make presents and pay "customary fees" to superior officials and their personnel every time he had dealings with them, besides "door fees" to gate porters, "tea money" to runners and personal servants, and so on and so forth. But where did he and his colleagues get the necessary money for all these expenses? The answer is very simple. It was done by the same methods as those used for collecting fees for every imaginable occasion. "Customary fees" is a euphemistic translation of the prudish term *lou-kuei*[c24] (lit. "base custom" or "vile practice"), which simply means bribes, and bribery was a custom which pervaded every office from top to bottom and which impregnated every rank of society. To give an idea of the variety and omnipresence of these "customary fees", I need name only a few. *Magistrates* regularly collected an allowance from taxpayers to make up for the silver lost in the process of casting pieces into ingots, this being called a "meltage fee" or "fee for meltage loss" (*huo-hao*).[c25] It varied from ten to fifty per cent of the tax itself. Moreover, the magistrates took copper coins instead of silver, at a conversion rate higher than the market rate; demanded extra silver for land tax payments, and commodities in kind without payment or at an "official price" lower than the market price; exacted fees from their own yamen personnel—clerks, scribes, and runners—every time they were assigned to a lucrative job or mission; and, in general, exacted money from all the people under their jurisdiction (a) for everything the commoners desired to obtain, and (b) for everything the commoners wished to escape from.

On a lower level, the picture was even worse. Clerks exacted "money for pens and paper", fees for registration and for handling a complaint, fees for the endorsement of a case, for the issue of a warrant, for a trial, for attending the court, for investigations, for the withdrawal or the conclusion of a lawsuit, for issuing tax notices and tax receipts, and for every stage in the collection of tribute grain and miscellaneous taxes, frequently charging the taxpayer several times for the same operation.

Government runners, in close co-operation with the government clerks, received bribes from people involved in a lawsuit, from people suspected in a murder case, and when they were sent to rural zones to collect taxes, or when they served in granaries. From persons being arrested or summoned they demanded

money for "shoes and socks", wine and meal money, boat

and carriage fare, and money for hiring a donkey. The runners also collected fees from both plaintiff and defendant for bringing them to court for a trial. The plaintiff and defendant were not allowed to see the magistrate or to go home until an agreed sum had been paid. A convicted criminal also had to pay a fee for being taken to the superior yamen for retrial.[11]

Needless to say, personal servants, sitting in the centre of the spider's web, had a fat share of all the "customary fees". But it is impossible and unnecessary to enumerate here all kinds of "base practices". You can find all the desired information in the book by Prof. Ch'ü T'ung-tsu to which I referred at the beginning of my lecture. The point which I wish to take up is the distinction which Ch'ü tries to make between "customary fees" (an established custom in China) and "corrupt practices"—the latter being an intensification of the former. In other words, he tries to establish a dividing line between what might be called *legal corruption*—that is, corruption which is accepted or tolerated—and *illegal, punishable corruption*. He does not, in my opinion, succeed in doing so, for he seems to me to refute his own argument as soon as he has stated it:

Although the practice was, as the term suggests, "irregular" and "low", it was nevertheless established and authorized and became widely accepted. It was thus within toleration of the law. It should not be confused with bribery and other forms of corruption, which were unlawful and prohibited. *However, in some cases there was no sharp dividing line between the collection of a customary fee and corruption. . . . It was difficult to define just what constituted legitimate administrative expenses and how much was actually needed for them.* Officials and yamen personnel soon began to abuse the practice of *lou-kuei* and created a serious administrative problem for the government. *The variety of the fees increased, and so did the amounts.* The whole matter was beyond the control of the government, especially the central government, which had *no way of knowing even the different types*

> *of customary fees in use in various localities, let alone*
> *any way of checking their use.*[12] (Italics added.)

This excellent statement requires, however, to be slightly modified if it is to be brought into relation with the facts. I would go so far as to say that there *never* was a dividing line between ordinary bribes and extraordinary corruption and that it is impossible to define their respective limits, since *corruption was part of the normal, ordinary, institutionalized way of life.* Those who study the under-developed countries of today can perhaps appreciate this remark.

But let us return once again to Wang Hui-tsu. His experience seems to bear out the standard accusation of corruption amongst clerks, runners, and personal servants. His general recommendation is that they should be treated firmly and with severity, but that they should not be pushed around, and special care should be taken to prevent them from losing face, especially in the case of the older, experienced men, who are more reliable than the youngsters who show all too much eagerness and zeal. (82, 83, 84) However, to underline the importance of personal servants, and in particular the importance of the gate-porter and of the attendant who deals with the endorsement of documents, either of whom could have effect on the magistrate's reputation and career, he tells a story about one of his former servants whom he hired, believing him to be trustworthy, for the all-important post of gate-porter. A year later, the man was accused of irregular conduct and of accepting bribes, with deleterious effect on official business, entailing blackmail and the postponement in the delivery, or failure to deliver, documents, etc. Wang refused to believe it, and kept the porter on for another year until his guilt was finally disclosed. (12, 13) In short, one easily gets the impression that those innocent angels, the officials, were surrounded by a hydra of "mean people". This is no doubt true. But it is also true that all the most confidential jobs were entrusted to personal servants who acted as intermediaries between the magistrate and his staff and co-ordinated the various activities of secretaries, clerks, and runners, although not allowed to contact each other directly, and who, last but not least, were used as go-betweens in dealing with other yamen and more especially with higher officials. According to Ch'ü T'ung-tsu, "not a single document could pass through the clerks of the superior yamen without a payment".[13] Personal servants, who were usually not natives of the locality where the magistrate was stationed, sometimes acquired considerable wealth. Wang Hui-tsu advises newly appointed young magistrates who have just arrived in a new place and find themselves short of funds, to borrow money from private secretaries and servants. (14) And he also mentions the custom—at first sight difficult to understand—whereby runners and personal servants offered money to a magistrate in order to be taken into his service. It was a good investment. All these people had a key position in the intricate, well-oiled, and all-embracing machinery of corruption.

To suggest that everything was corrupt in this society is perhaps an exaggeration which provides a caricature of Chinese bureaucracy. But after all, a caricature often portrays essential features better than a photograph can do. In any case, no one can fail to ask the question: how could such a machinery work? Well, it worked badly, but it worked somehow. I would even go so far as to adopt the view of Ho Ping-ti, which is not explicitly stated in his book on population, but which is nevertheless implied as one of the main results of his researches—namely, that during the eighteenth century, China, under the Manchu dynasty, and before the massive impact of Europe, perhaps enjoyed one of the happiest and most peaceful ages in all its long history. Or to put this in a way that is perhaps nearer to the truth, this might be said to be one of the least unhappy periods in Chinese history.

One final word. It should be remembered that the "Opinions on apprenticeship in government" is only one of Wang Hui-tsu's works, and that there are at least a dozen other guides for officials. This particular text is one of the most difficult I have ever come across, and when sweating over my translation, I have several times had moments of despair when I nearly decided to give up the attempt. (The incredible inadequacy of our existing dictionaries was time and again borne in on me.) My translation is still unfinished, and it needs patience and perseverance. There is still much to be done in this unpoetic, and for many people unattractive field. In spite of the difficulties, I remain convinced that this is a task which must be undertaken and that it will yield results we cannot do without.

Fontenay-aux-Roses, 5 to 11 January 1963

NOTES

Lecture I

1. Nelson J. Wu, "Tung Ch'i-ch'ang (1555-1636): Apathy in Government and Fervor in Art", in *Confucian Personalities*, ed. A. F. Wright and D. Twitchett (Stanford, 1962), pp. 260-93.
2. Wu, pp. 260-1.
3. *Shih-chi*, ch. 66.
4. Trans. by Wm. Theodore de Bary, in *Sources of Chinese Tradition* (Columbia University Press, 1960), pp. 587-8. (The end of the final sentence has been altered.)
5. *Ibid.*, pp. 589-90 (with a few slight alterations).
6. *Ibid.*, pp. 591-2.
7. *Ibid.*, pp. 597.
8. Trans. based on that by W. T. de Bary in *A plan for the prince*: the *Ming-i tai-fang lu* trans. and explained ... Ann Arbor University Microfilms (1954), publication 6599.
9. W. T. de Bary, "Chinese Despotism and the Confucian Ideal: A Seventeenth Century View", in *Chinese Thought and Institutions*, ed. J. K. Fairbank (Chicago, 1957), pp. 179-80.

Lecture II

1. Or perhaps: "widely versed in letters", or: "in your studies make use of the widest range of sources"; *Lun-yü* VI.25.
2. *Lun-yü* XIII.20.
3. Trans. by W. T. de Bary, in *Sources of Chinese Tradition*, pp. 608-10 (with a few slight alterations).
4. *T'ing-lin yü-chi* 26b, first of Six Letters to P'an Tz'u-keng. (*Ssu-pu ts'ung-kan.* 1st series.)
5. From *Jih-chih lu chi-shih* (*Ssu-pu pei-yao*) 9.15a-16a, trans. by W. T. Bary in *Sources of Chinese Tradition*, p. 611. (The last sentence has been expanded.)
6. *T'ing-lin wen-chi* (*Ssu-pu ts'ung-k'an*, 1st series) 1.7a-12b.
7. Trans. by W. T. de Bary, in *Sources of Chinese Tradition*, pp. 611-12 (with a few slight alternations).
8. *Jih-chih lu* 18.
9. *T'ing-lin shih-chi* (*Ssu-pu ts'ung-k'an*, 1st series) 5.17a.
10. *Sung-lun* (*Ssu-pu pei-yao*) 7.1a.

11. Trans. by W. T. de Bary, in *Sources of Chinese Tradition*, pp. 604-05 (with a few slight alterations).
12. *Tu T'ung-chien lun (Ssu-pu pei-yao)* 5.9a.
13. *Tu T'ung-chien lun* 7.
14. *Ibid.* 28.13a-b, trans. by W. T. de Bary, in *Sources of Chinese Tradition*, pp. 602-3 (with a few slight alterations).
15. *Tu T'ung-chien lun* 3.
16. *Ibid.* 4.2a.
17. *Ssu-wen lu wai-p'ien.*
18. *Huang-shu* 1. Trans. by W. T. de Bary, in *Sources of Chinese Tradition*, pp. 601-2.

Lecture III
1. Harvard East Asian Studies, 1959.
2. Seattle, 1960.
3. Harvard East Asian Studies, 1962.
4. London School of Economics Monographs on Social Anthropology, 1962.
5. Trans. by C. K. Yang in "Chinese Bureaucratic Behavior" (in *Confucianism in Action*, ed. D. S. Nivison and A. F. Wright, Stanford. 1959, pp. 134-64), pp. 156-7.
6. *Ibid.*, p. 157.
7. *Ibid.*, p. 158.
8. *Ibid.*, p. 155.
9. Vol. I, pp. 32-35.
10. Trans. by D. H. Nivison, in "Ho-shen and his accusers" (*Confucianism in Action*, pp. 209-43), pp. 216-17, with slight alterations.
11. Ch'ü T'ung-tsu, *Local Government in China under the Ch'ing*, pp. 65-6.
12. *Ibid.*, pp. 26-7.
13. *Ibid.*, p. 46.

A complete bibliography of Professor Balazs' writings can be found appended to the obituary by Professor Demiéville published in *T'oung Pao LI*, 2/3 (1964), pp. 247-61.

Lecture I

(1) 理學
(2) 漢學
(3) 考證
(4) 一條鞭法
(5) 市鎮
(6) 五雜俎
(7) 市民
(8) 市豪
(9) 明史
(10) 工部徵賈須知
(11) 梅
(12) 水滸傳
(13) 李贄(卓吾)
(14) 金瓶梅
(15) 王世禎
(16) 三言:馮夢龍
(17) 拍案驚奇:凌濛初
(18) 今古奇觀(人瑞)
(19) 李漁(笠翁)
(20) 拍案肉蒲
(21) 金聖歎(人瑞)
(22) 西廂記
(23) 書院
(24) 復社案成
(25) 狂禪
(26) 董其昌
(27) 萬曆神宗
(28) 挺擊自
(29) 紅丸案
(30) 移宮案
(31) 魏忠賢
(32) 李自成(黎洲)
(33) 桂王
(34) 石濤
(35) 黃宗羲(黎洲)
(36) 劉宗周
(37) 爾八山人,勾踐殺爾父乎?
(38) 小東林魯學
(39) 阮大鋮
(40) 南都訪錄
(41) 福王
(42) 東浙學派
(43) 明夷待訪錄
(44) 明儒學案
(45) 浙自利
(46) 章學誠
(47) 原君
(48) 自私
(49) 自利
(50) 主,客
(51) 原臣
(52) 原法
(53) 無法之法
(54) 非法之法
(55) 井田
(56) 明會典
(57) 學校
(58) 語錄

Lecture II

(1) 顧炎武(亭林)
(2) 心,性
(3) 危微精一
(4) 博學於文
(5) 行己有恥
(6) 天下郡國利病書
(7) 亭林餘集,潘耒(次耕)(1646-1708)
(8) 明史稿
(9) 明史輯略
(10) 音學五書
(11) 肇域志
(12) 日知

論人方外論從卽，之自兵夷固，自

員聖棱生叛剛敢於彌剪去憤詩悲憤義

⟨16⟩錢糧之無忌難我庵尚書引義鑑論忠全之理論非以不社

⟨15⟩錢糧之無忌難我續夢 ⟨21⟩書引義鑑之孤辛理者勢叙論 ⟨35⟩以能施

⟨14⟩郡縣小人嗟 ⟨18⟩ ⟨20⟩續書夢 ⟨24⟩尚讀通石之企勢理者理也 ⟨22⟩周易宋命於然理之寓施

⟨13⟩封建自古于李之⟨夫之⟩ 遺書夢 ⟨28⟩讀越不能音之勢 ⟨34⟩敘道類之

建古李山⟨夫之⟩山遺書 ⟨27⟩噩墓：抱而勢必天下 ⟨39⟩族

錄 ⟨17⟩愚按莫甚王船山 ⟨23⟩船山夫之世 ⟨31⟩順之必天人相於之 ⟨40⟩船山學社

⟨30⟩明遺臣王夫之正學而 ⟨32⟩順郡縣者人與人羣也

致固當然者 ⟨36⟩信義保仁義 ⟨38⟩雲云云哉？

希衡則天也 ⟨37⟩保他

當然者農也

然於狄而何

Lecture III

⟨1⟩ 政書要略 ⟨2⟩ 職官舉要，須知 ⟨3⟩ 官制便覽 ⟨4⟩ 官箴 ⟨5⟩ 指南 南祖

⟨6⟩ 學治臆說 ⟨7⟩ 汪輝 輝言

⟨8⟩ 史姓韻編 ⟨9⟩ 佐治藥言 續佐治藥言 ⟨10⟩

學治續說 學治說贅 ⟨11⟩ 知州知縣 ⟨12⟩ 父母

官 ⟨13⟩ 棍匪 ⟨14⟩ 待罪 ⟨15⟩ 聖賢 ⟨16⟩ 訟師 師 ⟨17⟩

城隍神 ⟨18⟩ 地方土神 ⟨19⟩ 各鄉土地神 地 ⟨20⟩

保 ⟨21⟩ 法理 ⟨22⟩ 情 ⟨23⟩ 養廉銀 ⟨24⟩ 陋規 ⟨25⟩

火耗

INDEX